1982
Official
World's Fair
Cookbook

Knoxville, Tenn.
May—Oct 1982

Recipes Specially
Selected, Compiled & Edited
for the World's Fair
by
Phila Hach

5th Printing

Recipes Selected
from Phila Hach's previous cookbooks
Kitchen Kollege Copyright 1956
From Phila with Love Copyright 1973
Kountry Kooking Copyright 1974
The United Nations Cookbook 1980
ISBN 0-9606192-0-8
Published 1981
by
Phila Hach
1601 Madison St.
Clarksville, Tenn. 37040

Distributed by
Joe K. Hach

Welcome to the 1982 World's Fair

Ideas are the common province of all men. Nations and societies seem to flourish or decline in proportion to the imaginative and creative thoughts of the people who compose them. This "Energy" oriented meeting of the great nations of the world places focus on man's creative thinking and planning toward a better future for our world. Man has taken those eternal gifts of sun and wind and turned them into working tools to make life better for all humanity. This world's fair will bring into reality the hopes and progress that lie ahead in the fields of Chemistry, Electricity, Mechanics and Atomic Energy. Because of today's research tomorrow will be a better place for all peoples of the universe.

We hope this little Cookbook will be a happy reminder of your visit to Tennessee and will express our warm and sincere greetings to each of you.

From all of us at The 1982 World's Fair

Phila R. Hach

To Marg and Dave
Love and Happy Cooking
Phila R. Hach

ABOUT THE AUTHOR

Phila Rawlings Hach attended the University of Tennessee, received her degree in music from Ward-Belmont College and later her degree in foods and nutrition from Vanderbilt University and Peabody College for Teachers.

After graduation from college, Phila joined American Airlines as a stewardess and later became a Supervisor of Training for the company. She did special research in holding foods at high altitudes and compiled an in-flight food manual for the airline industry. While with American, she collected recipes from country homes around the world.

In the early 1950's she joined the staff of WSM-TV and for years conducted a very popular homemakers' show, "Kitchen Kollege". She was the recipient of The National Zenith Television Award for outstanding contributions to public service programming and was twice selected Cook-of-the-Month by "The Chicago Tribune". She is listed in the first edition of "Who's Who of Living American Women".

Phila is the author of four previous cookbooks, "Kitchen Kollege", recipes from her T.V. show. "From Phila with Love" an inspirational and intimate collection of recipes from their famous Inn; "Kountry Kooking", Oprylands official cookbook and one of the most celebrated books on down on the farm cooking; her last book, "Phila Hach's United Nations Cookbook" is a great collection of international favorites from the U.N. Ambassadors.

In compiling recipes for the 1982 Worlds Fair Cookbook, she has selected the most sought after recipes from the South, combining regional and Southern recipes with International favorites.

APPETIZERS
SOUPS

ITALIAN BLESSING

May your life
Be like good wine
Tasty, sharp and clear,
And like good wine
May it improve
With every passing year.

. . An Italian Blessing

Vegetable Beef Soup
International

1½ pounds shin bone of beef
1 pound stew beef
3 quarts cold water
½ teaspoon peppercorns, crushed
3 whole cloves
2 bay leaves
1 teaspoon whole thyme rubbed to a powder
2 teaspoons whole marjoram rubbed to a powder

2 sprigs parsley
2 cans tomatoes (No. 2½)
1 can tomato juice (No. 2)
4 carrots sliced
1 parsnip sliced
2 turnips cubed
2 onions diced
3 cups chopped celery
2 potatoes diced
2 tablespoons salt
2 tablespoons celery seed

Simmer bone, beef and water 3 hours. Take out bone and add rest of ingredients. Simmer gently 2 hours. This makes a nice clear vegetable beef soup.

Vichysoisse
French

6 onions, chopped
2 cups thinly sliced potatoes
4 cups chicken bouillon

1 cup cream
Salt and white pepper to taste
2 tablespoons minced parsley

⅓ cup butter

Cook potatoes and onion. Add rest of ingredients. Simmer until thick. Serve hot or ice cold.

White Bean Soup
Southern

1 bay leaf
1 pound navy beans
1 stalk or bunch celery

6 carrots (large)
4 medium sized onions
1 No. 2½ can tomatoes

1 ham hock

Soak navy beans in water overnight. Put soaked beans, ham hock and rest of ingredients in heavy pot with plenty of water to cover. Simmer gently for three hours or until done. Add water as necessary to keep vegetables covered. If needed, add salt and pepper.

Pepper Pot
Southern

1 bunch celery, chopped
6 green peppers
4 tomatoes (No. 2½ can)
4 leeks
3 raw potatoes, medium
¼ cup rice
4 finely chopped onions

¼ pound ham (diced)
¾ pound cooked, diced tripe
Black pepper and salt to taste
½ teaspoon marjoram
¼ teaspoon ground sage
1 bay leaf
1 gallon beef broth

Saute all vegetables in butter. Place in soup pot and add 1 gallon beef broth. Add tripe, rice, ham and seasoning. Simmer until thick, about 1½ hours. Whole peppercorns are good in this soup. Makes 10 servings.

Buttermilk Soup
Libya

1 lb. potatoes
1 tablespoon flour
1 quart buttermilk

3 strips bacon
1 onion, peeled and chopped
Salt and pepper

Scrub potatoes, rinse, drain, pare and chop. Cover with salted water and cook until tender. Drain; mix flour smoothly with a little buttermilk. Stir into rest of buttermilk. Bring to a boil. Chop bacon and cook with onion until brown. Combine potatoes, hot buttermilk, flour mixture, bacon and onion. Season with salt and pepper.

Cracker crumbs (Approx. 2 cups)
4 eggs
3 tablespoons chicken fat
4 half-egg shells of water
Salt, pepper and minced parsley
Dash nutmeg

Beat eggs, then add chicken fat, water and seasonings to taste. Add sufficient cracker crumbs to make stiff dough. Shape into small balls and drop into boiling chicken broth that has been flavored generously with parsley. Let boil for 30 minutes.

3 pounds fresh fish
2 slices salt pork
2 slices onion
5 potatoes, diced
½ pint coffee cream
Salt and pepper to taste

Cover fish with water and simmer until it flakes. Remove fish from kettle. Add salt pork and cook for 3 minutes. Take out and render in skillet. Add onions and cook until brown. (Meanwhile boil cubed potatoes in fish stock.) When potatoes are done pour fish and onion in mixture and simmer for 15 minutes. Add coffee cream. Serve piping hot.

1 pound bones
1 pound stew meat
1 carrot
4 potatoes
1 rutabaga
2 small onions
4 celery tops
1½ quarts water
1 can No. 2 tomatoes
1 can tomato puree
Salt and pepper to taste
Handful parsley

NOODLES:
1 cup unsifted flour
1 egg
Pinch salt
⅛ teaspoon cream tartar
½ egg shell of water

Put bones, stew beef and water in a soup pot and cook until beef is tender. Then add other ingredients and simmer gently until done. About two hours. Stuff noodles and drop into boiling soup and cook vigorously for about 20 minutes.

Make well in flour and fill with ingredients. Work the ingredients in gently to form a soft workable dough. Then roll dough out on a floured board to a thin sheet.

STUFFING:
1 pound ground beef
1 egg
1 small onion diced
Bunch parsley, chopped
Salt and pepper to taste
Bread crumbs if desired

Combine all ingredients and spread over entire sheet of noodle dough. Cut the stuffing covered dough in 1 inch strips. Starting at the top of 1 strip, fold over about 1 inch, cut off, pinch sides together and drop in boiling soup. Continue until all the dough is used up.

Hard cooked eggs sliced with a dab of caviar or anchovy paste are a real good nibbling teaser! Don't forget salted nuts and cubes of good cheese - Bel Paese and Cheddar.
A few more goodies before the main course -
Strips of fresh vegetables - squash, carrots, broccoli, cauliflower, cucumbers and celery. Crisp in ice water.

Lentil Soup
Saudi Arabia

1/2 cup lentils
2 cups onion, coarsely chopped
2 teaspoons salt
2 quarts (8 cups) boiling water

1 cup chopped Swiss Chard
   or spinach
2 tablespoons olive oil
Juice of 1/2 lemon

Cleanse lentils thoroughly and put into salted water. Add onions and mix. Cook over medium fire for one hour or until the lentils are tender. Add Swiss chard or spinach, olive oil, and lemon juice.

If it is desired, one pound of 1/2" cubed lamb can be added with the lentils. The lamb should be lean. Simmer as for the lentils over medium heat. Stir thoroughly before serving. Lamb should always be cooked slowly.

Cucumber Buttermilk Soup
Southern

2 10 oz. cans mushroom soup
2 cups buttermilk
1 cup minced seeded cucumbers

1/2 cup minced celery
2 tablespoons minced green onions

Mix all together and chill. Serve with a dab of sour cream and paprika.

Banana Soup
Ivory Coast

1 quart orange juice
5 ripe bananas
2 cups whole milk

2 oz. kirsch
nutmeg to taste (1/2 teaspoon)

Blend all ingredients. Chill thoroughly and serve with a dab of whipped cream and finely chopped roasted peanuts.

Stuffed Celery
Southern

8 ounce package cream cheese
1¼ ounces Roquefort cheese
¼ teaspoon garlic salt
½ cup chopped pecans

2 tablespoons mayonnaise
A little milk to make right consistency.

Mix all ingredients well. Stuff celery or use as a spread for potato chips or crackers.

Coconut Chips
Hawaii

1 coconut

Salt to taste

Drain milk from coconut. Cut in thin strips. Toast in a 250° oven for 4 hours. Remove from oven and sprinkle with salt.

Cereal Nut Crunch
Southern

½ cup margarine
1 teaspoon Worcestershire
   sauce
½ teaspoon onion or garlic salt
½ teaspoon salt
2 cups cheerios

2 cups kix
2 cups wheat chex
2 cups rice chex
2 cups pretzels (broken)
2 cups cheese tidbits
1½ cups mixed salted nuts

Mix all ingredients together and toast for one hour in a 250° oven. Stir every 15 minutes with a wooden spoon.

1/4 cup chopped onion
1/4 cup butter
4 cups chicken broth
1 can evaporated milk

1 cup canned pumpkin
1 teaspoon salt
1/2 teaspoon black pepper
3 tablespoons flour

Cream of Pumpkin Soup
Rwanda

Saute onion and butter in large saucepan. Add 4 cups chicken broth and canned milk and pumpkin. Simmer for 20 minutes. Do not boil. Season with salt and pepper. Serve hot!

---

1 cup cooked shrimp
   (do not over cook)
1/2 cup chopped oysters
1/2 cup minced celery hearts
2 cups milk

1 cup cream
1/4 cup butter
Dash of Tabasco Sauce
Salt and black pepper to taste
¼ cup flour

Seafood Bisque
Southern

Melt butter and blend in flour in top of double boiler; gradually add milk and cream. Stir until smooth. Ten minutes before serving, add minced celery and chopped shrimp and oysters. Season with salt, pepper and Tabasco. Serve in cups with a dash of whipped cream sprinkled with paprika. (Makes about 6 servings.)

Cook dried beans until soft. Drain well and season to taste with chopped onions, chopped ginger and hot red pepper and salt. Shape into balls and roll in self-rising cornmeal. Drop into hot fat and fry until golden brown. Serve hot!

Bean Fritters
Africa

Ingredients:
  4 medium onions
  3 tablespoons chicken base
  3 teaspoons Maggi seasoning
  2 tablespoons melted butter
  3 tablespoons salt
  1 tablespoon black pepper
  3 quarts water

1/4 cup Sherry
3 tablespoons flour
Bread Crumb Toppinig:
  1 cup breadcrumbs
  1 teaspoon paprika
  1 teaspoon melted butter
  1 ounce old English cheese

French Onion Soup
Serves 6-8
French

Preparation:
Melt butter in two-gallon pot. Saute onions until transparent. Add Maggi seasoning, chicken base, flour, and mix well. Add water, bring to a boil and return to simmer for 20 minutes. Remove from heat and add Sherry.
Serving Suggestions:
pour soup into bowl. Place small crouton with melted mozzarella cheese, cheeseside down in soup. Completely cover top of bowl with sliced mozzarella cheese so that all areas of the lip of the bowl are covered. Sprinkle with breadcrumbs and cheese topping. Place in oven until cheese melts and breadcrumb mixture is golden brown. May be served with garlic bread toast.

½ Avocado - French dressing
½ broiled grapefruit with
  sherry or rum

½ dozen cold oysters on half shell
  with lemon juice, horseradish
  and catsup

Universal Favorites

Apricot Soup
Belgium

3/4 lb. dried apricots
3 ripe fresh peaches
1/4 lb. fresh cherries

5 cups water
1/2 cup sugar
1/4 cup tapioca

Wash apricots in warm water. Combine with rest of fruit. Add water and sugar. Let stand overnight. Next day, cook fruit in water it was soaked in. Strain through a sieve. Heat to boiling point. Add the tapioca, gradually, and cook until soup is thick and clear. Remove from heat and stir in the juice of 1 lemon. Serve warm or cold.

Blueberry Soup
German

1 1/2 cups blueberries, washed
1 quart water
1/4 cup sugar

2 tablespoons cornstarch
3 tablespoons water

Place in saucepan 1 quart of water with the blueberries. Bring to boil and simmer until very soft. Strain berries through fine sieve, and return to the saucepan. Mix cornstarch and water, add to soup and cook until thickens. Stir adding 1/4 cup sugar. Simmer 3 minutes. Chill and serve.

Anchovy Cheese
Hungary

1 1/2 sticks butter
8 ounces cream cheese
1/2 can beer
2 tablespoons paprika

1 can anchovies
1 tablespoon Worcestershire Sauce
1 tablespoon grated onion

Mix all ingredients together. Serve with crackers!

Steak Tartare
(Raw Beef Appetizer)
International

1 lb. finely ground beef tenderloin
1 raw egg
1/2 cup finely chopped parsley
2 teaspoon poupon mustard
1 clove garlic minced

1 small onion minced
dash of worcestershire sauce
2 tablespoon capers
1 1/2 teaspoon salt
coarsely cracked pepper

Mix thoroughly until very smooth. Make into a nice round ball and serve with melba toast.

Cheese Pecan Wafers
United States

1 lb sharp cheddar cheese
1/2 tsp salt
2 1/4 cups flour

1 stick butter
1/2 tsp hot red pepper

Grate cheese and mix with butter. Let stand in warm spot of kitchen until soft and pliable. Mix in rest of ingredients and blend well. Shape into balls the size of marbles. Place on cookie sheet (use a damp cheese cloth stretched over a small glass to press balls into rounds). Place a pecan half into each wafer and bake 30 minutes in a 300° oven or until brown. Delicious.

2 pounds cooked chicken breast, cut in chunks
3 quarts chicken stock (simmer chicken bones for 6 hours in earthen pot)
1¾ teaspoon curry powder
1 cup diced cooked carrots
¼ cup diced cooked onion
1 large bay leaf

6 sprigs parsley
3 whole cloves
1 large eggplant, peeled, cut in squares and boiled in saltwater

Mulligatawny
India

Have all vegetables cooked. Add vegetables, chicken and ingredients. Simmer 30 minutes. Stir in 1 pint rich cream sauce. Serve immediately with fluffy rice.

---

1 bunch fresh beets
1 quart boiling water
1 egg yolk

1 pint sour cream
1 tablespoon fresh lemon juice
1½ teaspoon salt

Cold Beet Soup
Russia

Wash beets thoroughly and then cook them in boiling water for 20-30 minutes. Reserve liquid. Peel and grate or sliver beets. Mix egg yolk and sour cream. Cool beets and water they were cooked in. Fold the two together and add lemon juice and salt. Serve ice cold.

---

2 cups clam juice
2 cups chicken broth
1 pint heavy cream
1 tablespoon chopped dill or dill seed
2 tablespoons chopped chives

2 tablespoons minced parsley
Onion salt
Celery salt
2 to 3 tablespoons cornstarch
2/3 cup gin

Gin Soup
Europe

Dissolve cornstarch in a little water. Mix other ingredients, except gin and cornstarch, and bring to a boil. Thicken soup with cornstarch mixture. Add gin, bring to a boil and let simmer a few minutes. Season to taste. Serve hot or cold.

½ cup oil
1 medium onion, sliced
1 chopped leek
1 sliced tomato
1 sliced carrot
1 clove garlic
3 pounds fish (boneless), cut in 1½ inch pieces
1 can lobster or 1 pound fresh

1 can clams or 2 dozen fresh (shelled)
1 quart water
1/3 cup lemon juice
1 teaspoon salt
1/8 teaspoon pepper
1 tablespoon minced parsley
1 teaspoon soy sauce

Bouillabaisse Martinique
Martinique

Saute onion in oil; cook until transparent. Add leek, tomato, carrot and garlic. Add fish, water, lemon juice, salt, pepper and parsley. Season to taste with soy sauce. Simmer 30 minutes.

---

3 strips bacon (cut in small pieces)
½ cup sliced mushrooms
2 cloves garlic
¼ cup chopped green onion
¼ cup chopped bell pepper
½ lb. boiled shrimp, diced
1 pint oysters

½ cup lemon juice
½ cup sherry
¼ cup parsley
Thick cream sauce (2 cups)
Cracker crumbs
Oyster shells

Oysters Bienville
Southern

Saute bacon, mushrooms, garlic, onion and pepper. Combine lemon juice, sherry and parsley. Add to skillet with bacon. Stir and thicken with a little cornstarch. Combine with thick cream sauce. Add shrimp pieces, place oysters on shells, cover with shrimp sauce. Sprinkle with crumbs and dot with butter. Broil until bubbly hot.

3 pounds top of round (chopped)   3 quarts cold water
(Never use fatty meat or bones if
a clear soup is desired.)

French Bouillon
France

1 onion, cut in quarters   2 whole cloves
1 carrot, cut lengthwise   Dash salt
2 whole stalks of celery with leaves   Strips of lemon rind (1 lemon)
1 big sprig parsley   Cayenne pepper
1 bay leaf   ¼ teaspoon celery seed
1 teaspoon peppercorns

Let meat stand in 3 quarts cold water for 1 hour. Set on stove and simmer *(below boiling)* for 24 hours. (This is important.)

Next morning add onion, carrot, celery, parsley, bay leaf, peppercorns and cloves. Continue to simmer for 4 hours. Chill in refrigerator overnight. Next morning strain soup.

Add strips of lemon rind, cayenne pepper and salt to taste and celery seed. Simmer 1 hour and serve.

Jamaica Pepperpot (Hot and Spicy)
Jamaica

1 pound kale, ground   1 quart chicken stock
1 pound cabbage, ground   ½ teaspoon salt
1½ pounds beef, cubed and cooked   ⅛ teaspoon cayenne
½ pound cooked chicken   ½ teaspoon thyme
½ pound cooked corned beef   2 green onions, sliced
1 cup coconut   1 pod garlic
12 okra, cut   2 tablespoons Worcestershire sauce
2 onions, ground

Combine all ingredients except okra. Cook over low heat for 1½ hours. Add okra and continue cooking until tender.

Senegalese
Asia

2 cups cream sauce   ¾ teaspoon curry powder
4 egg yolks   Salt to taste
3½ cups chicken broth (canned)   1 cup cooked breast of chicken

Combine and cook over low heat until it thickens. Combine with cream, egg yolk mixture. Chill and serve with chives.

Gazpacho
Spanish

1 cup chopped celery   ½ cup chopped fresh spinach
1 cup chopped scallions   1 teaspoon fresh chopped basil
1 cup peeled, chopped cucumbers   ½ teaspoon fresh dill
1 cup chopped green bell peppers   ¼ cup chopped black olives
2 cups diced, firm ripe tomatoes   Salt to taste
2 cups jellied consomme

Combine all ingredients and chill until cold, cold, cold. Serve in soup cups with a slice of lemon and fresh ground pepper.

Escargots (36 Snails)
France

Allow 6 snails per person. (We use canned snails.)

Prepare snail butter as follows:

1 cup soft butter   Dash of Tabasco
½ teaspoon garlic powder   Seasoning salt to taste
1 teaspoon chives

Blend ingredients. Force butter mixture into snail shell. Place in snail - dab a little more butter at end. Run in broiler until hot and bubbly. Serve hot with French rolls.

¼ pound ground cooked ham
¼ pound ground cooked pork

¼ pound ground cooked corned beef

3 tablespoons shortening
1 cup flour
1 teaspoon dry mustard

1 teaspoon onion salt
1 cup milk
1 pound can chopped sauerkraut
　　(drained)

Sauerkraut Balls
Poland

Combine meats and add to thick sauce made by mixing shortening, flour, seasonings and milk. Stir in drained sauerkraut, chopped.

Shape paste into small balls (bite size). Fry in hot fat after dipping in egg and cracker crumbs. These are very popular cocktail treats! Serve Hot.

---

2 cups chopped fresh parsley
3 cloves garlic
¼ cup fresh basil (1 tsp. dry)
2 tablespoons wine vinegar
¼ cup chopped anchovies

Black cracked pepper
3 tablespoons oil
¼ cup pimento
3 tablespoons capers

Anchovy Sauce (Cold) For Antipasto
Italian

Combine all ingredients. Toss with whole pitted black olives, sliced. Arrange vegetables - hearts of palm, whole fresh mushrooms, whole green beans, chunks of tuna, small gherkins and hard cooked eggs - on platter with strips of prosciutto. Pour over anchovy sauce. Serve with crackers.

½ pound cream cheese
4 ounces blue cheese
1 pound processed cheese
2 tablespoons beer or sherry

1 tablespoon prepared mustard
½ teaspoon garlic powder
½ teaspoon salt

Cheese Log
English

Beat the 3 cheeses together. Add rest of ingredients. Shape into log and roll in chives and paprika. Serve with crackers.

---

1 cucumber
1 cup cream cheese
1 teaspoon onion salt

Tint green food coloring
Homemade mayonnaise

Benedictine Filling
Southern

Blend ingredients together and spread on bread. Top with tiny wedge of fresh tomato. Sprinkle with dill, basil or chives.

---

1 cup raw scallops
1 cup raw shrimp

1 cup raw boneless fish (cubed)
2 peeled, sliced avocado

Cube fish, shrimp and avocado.

1 cup lime juice
¼ cup chopped green onions
2 tablespoons fresh chopped parsley
2 tablespoons chopped bell pepper
½ cup oil

½ teaspoon dried oregano
Dash Tabasco
1 teaspoon salt
Ground black peppercorns
¼ cup chopped pimento

Ceviche
South America

Marinate overnight in rest of ingredients, thoroughly mixed.* No, it isn't cooked by heat. The lime juice cooks the raw fish. This is terrific.

* Be sure and leave in marinade overnight, refrigerated.

ENTREES

THE finest fibre in a man's breast is represented by his true character.

A good character is worth more than a good bank account. Character can make a bank account but a bank account cannot make character.

Your character is what you build into your life through the principles for which you stand in your everyday work or play.

As a man thinks, so he lives — and so is his character.

We may misjudge or misunderstand each other in the ordinary course of events through an impulsive act or a rash remark — but true character is always revealed when the crucial test of loyalty, faith and trust is laid bare.

French Marinade

½ cup oil
1 tablespoon lemon juice
3 teaspoons sugar
1 cup red wine

½ teaspoon salt
½ teaspoon cracked pepper
½ teaspoon dried herbs -
  marjoram and thyme

Marinate filet mignon for at least 1 hour. Grill in half butter and half oil to desired doneness.

Brandy Glaze

¼ cup brandy
¼ cup water

2 tablespoons Worcestershire

Sprinkle with brandy glaze and coat both sides. Turn on hot grill and serve immediately.

Filet Mignon
French

Proceed as for filet above. Use the whole beef tenderloin, though. Grill whole tenderloin to desired doneness. Serve with sauce bearnaise and crisp bacon.

Sauce Bearnaise

2 shallots
2 tablespoons tarragon vinegar
4 egg yolks
1 teaspoon finely chopped parsley

4 tablespoons melted butter
1 tablespoon bouillon
½ teaspoon salt
1 teaspoon dried tarragon

Chop shallots. Heat with vinegar and let simmer a few minutes. Strain. Add egg yolks, 1 at a time, to vinegar, beating well. Add butter slowly with bouillon and seasoning. Stir well. Keep warm.

Chateaubriand
French

Butter Pastry

1½ cups pastry flour
½ teaspoon salt

1 stick butter
4 tablespoons ice water

Make pastry. Chill 1 hour. Roll out and place in pie pan.

Filling

1 cup grated Swiss cheese
4 eggs
2 cups cream
1 tablespoon cornstarch

Pinch of salt
Dash cayenne
1 teaspoon chopped onion

Combine first 7 ingredients. Pour into pie shell. Bake in 350 degree oven 25-30 minutes. Cut in pie wedges and serve.

Quiche Lorraine
French

3-5 pound red snapper (Dredge with
  flour - sprinkle with salt and
  pepper)

Place in baking dish.

Make sauce as follows:

6 tablespoons butter
½ cup chopped onion
2 cups chopped celery
¼ cup green pepper
3 cups canned tomatoes
1 tablespoon Worcestershire sauce

1 tablespoon catsup
1 teaspoon chili powder
½ lemon, sliced
2 bay leaves
1 clove garlic, minced
1 teaspoon salt

Saute onion, celery and pepper in butter for 15 minutes. Add rest of ingredients and simmer 15 minutes. Pour over red snapper and bake in 350 degree oven for about 45 minutes.

Baked Red Snapper
United States

Place rabbit in buttered baking dish and cover with following barbe Q sauce. Bake for 1½ hours at 350° or until tender.

Barbe-Q Rabbit
Southern

SAUCE:

1 tablespoon vinegar	1 teaspoon black pepper
1 tablespoon sugar	1 can bouillon
1 tablespoon dry mustard	1 medium minced onion
3 tablespoons Worcestershire sauce	2 cloves garlic, minced
½ bottle chili sauce or relish	¼ pound melted butter
1 teaspoon salt	2 drops liquid smoke (if desired)

Mix all ingredients and pour over meat.

---

1 fat hen	Dash of poultry seasoning
Handful parsley	Salt and pepper to taste
1 carrot	Water to cover

Stewed Chicken and Dumplings
Southern

Place hen in stewing kettle. Add parsley, carrot and poultry seasoning. Add a sprinkling of salt and pepper and water to cover. Simmer slowly until tender, about 4 hours. Save broth for dumplings.

DUMPLINGS:

2 cups flour	⅔ cup milk or a little more
4 teaspoons baking powder	½ teaspoon salt
	2 teaspoons butter

Mix and sift dry ingredients. Work in the butter with the tips of fingers. Add milk gradually. Roll out to a thickness of ¼ inches. Cut in strips of 1 inch by 2 inches. Drop in hot broth and cook from 8 to 10 minutes.

---

2 cups corn meal	3 tablespoons flour
¼ teaspoon salt	2 tablespoons chili powder
2 tablespoons fat	1 beaten egg
1½ cups boiling water	Corn husks

Hot Tamales
Mexico

Combine corn meal, salt and fat. Add boiling water and mix thoroughly. Add flour and chili powder. Add egg and mix well. Wash husks and soak in cold water for 2 or 3 hours. Spread about ¼ cup dough on husks to within 1 inch of edges. Spread dough with 2 tablespoons of tamale filling. Roll lengthwise edges of tamale to center, so they overlap. Wrap snugly in husk or parchment paper may be used. Fold up one inch at the end. Place tamales on rack and steam over hot water for 2 hours. Makes one dozen.

TAMALE FILLING:

1 clove garlic, minced	¾ cup tomato paste
¼ cup chopped onion	1 cup water
1 pound ground beef	1 teaspoon salt
	2 tablespoons chili powder

Cook garlic and onion in hot fat until done and yellow. Add remaining ingredients, cover and simmer for about 1¼ hours. Drain off fat.

2 onions, cut in slivers
2 small cloves of garlic
2 tablespoons fat
1½ pounds ground beef
6 cups water

6 tablespoons soy sauce
2 cans French style green
beans
5 tablespoons cornstarch
Cooked rice

Ow-Yok-Sung
Japan

Brown onion and minced garlic lightly in fat in heavy saucepan. Add ground beef and cook for 3 minutes, stirring to break up meat. Add water and soy sauce. Heat to boiling and add diced beans. Cook 10 minutes longer. Thicken with cornstarch mixed with a little water. Serve with rice.

---

1 domestic rabbit (3 pounds)
3 tablespoons butter
Salt and pepper to taste
¼ teaspoon nutmeg

1/16 teaspoon cayenne pepper
½ cup sauterne or sweet milk
1 tablespoon flour
1½ to 2 cups top milk

Fried Mr. Cotton Tail
Southern

Marinate rabbit in sauterne or milk for 30 minutes. Fry slowly in butter until tender and brown. Season to taste. Make gravy by adding flour to fat in skillet, blending well. Then pour in the top milk. Serve hot.

1½ cups chicken (slivered)
3 tablespoons peanut oil
½ cup ham slivered
½ cup thinly sliced onion
2 cups chopped celery
1 cup chopped green pepper

1 cup water
1 cup sliced mushrooms
½ cup chopped almonds
½ teaspoon salt
6 tablespoons soy sauce
2 tablespoons cornstarch

Chow Mein
China

Saute onion in oil. Add chicken, celery, pepper, etc. Cook for 5 minutes. Mix cornstarch with ¼ cup water and add to mixture. Add mushrooms and almonds. Serve with crisp noodles.

---

2 pounds beef, ground
¼ pound suet, ground
3 cloves garlic, ground
3 large potatoes, ground
3 onions, ground
1 cup tomato juice

3 tablespoons ground chili peppers
2 tablespoons flour
1 pound pinto beans, soaked overnight
Salt and pepper to taste

Chili
Mexico

Boil pinto beans in salted water until tender. Cook beef and suet in water enough to cover until it looses its red color and is done. Add rest of ingredients and cover with water to desired consistency. Simmer slowly for 1 hour. Stir often. For a thicker, more highly seasoned chili add: 1 pound ground pork, 2 cups tomato paste, 2 tablespoons chili powder, 1 teaspoon cumin, and 1 teaspoon oregano.

1½ cups rice—boil, drain
2 pounds shrimp
1 large onion
1 large bell pepper
1 clove garlic

1½ pounds tomatoes
1 teaspoon chili powder
⅛ teaspoon cayenne pepper
Salt and pepper to taste

Jambalaya
Southern

Saute onions and pepper in butter. Add rest of ingredients and cook about 15 minutes. Add rice that has been boiled.

2 cans tomatoes
1 pound white beans
Olive oil (4 teaspoons)
3 cloves garlic

1 pound macaroni, cooked
Pinch of sweet basil
Pork rind
Salt and pepper to taste

Pasta Fazioli
Italian

Soak white beans overnight. Put on to cook with pork rind and plenty of water. Cook gently for 2 hours or until tender. Saute garlic and basil in oil. Add tomatoes and cook about 10 minutes. Then add this to the beans. Next add the cooked macaroni, salt and pepper to taste.

1½ pounds ground beef
1 cup diced onions
1½ cup diced celery
1 cup diced raw potato

1 tablespoon flour
2 cans mock turtle soup or consomme
1 recipe for pie crust

Beef and Babble
English

Line baking pan with pie crust. Make alternate layers of meat and vegetables. Pour over the soup which has had the flour added. Top with pie crust and bake at 325° for 2 hours.

---

5 or 6 pounds spareribs
2 medium-sized onions, quartered
1 teaspoon salt
¼ teaspoon pepper
1 bay leaf
3 cloves
½ teaspoon mixed spices
⅛ teaspoon thyme
2 carrots, sliced thin

1 teaspoon English mustard
1 clove garlic, mashed
¼ cup vinegar
¼ cup sugar
3 cups chili sauce
½ cup A-1 sauce
½ cup Worcestershire sauce
Approximately 2 or 3 cups bouillon stock

Barbe-Q-Spareribs (Pork)
Southern

Place spareribs and onions in baking pan. Brown under broiler, turning to brown all sides. Tie spices in a small cheese cloth to keep them from going into sauce. Place in the pan with spareribs. Add carrots. Mix mustard, garlic, vinegar, sugar, chili sauce, A-1 sauce and Worcestershire sauce and pour over ribs. Add enough stock or bouillon to barely cover. Bring to a boil. Then set in a 350° oven and cook until well done, about 1½ hours. Remove spice bag before serving.

---

2 large onions, chopped
1/2 lb. butter
4 lbs. chopped beef
Salt and pepper to taste
Oregano
Dash garlic powder
1 2-lb. 3 ounce can Italian plum tomatoes
1 cup tomato puree or sauce

5-6 eggplants
Salt
6 eggs
4 cups milk
1/2 cup flour
1 teaspoon salt
2 tablespoons butter
Grated cheese

Moussaka
Greece

Brown onion in ¼ lb. of butter. Add ground beef and rest of seasonings, tomatoes and puree. Simmer for 1 hour stirring frequently. Slice eggplant and saute in rest of butter. Set aside. Blend rest of ingredients except cheese. Cook over low heat until thick. Make alternate layers of eggplant, meat mixture and sauce. End up with eggplant. Sprinkle with cheese. Bake 1 hour at 375°.

2 tablespoons oil
1½ pounds round steak, sliced diagonally in very thin slices
½ cup sugar
1⅛ cups soy sauce
1 cup water or mushroom stock
1 bunch green onions, cut in 1½ inch lengths (with tops)
2 cups bean sprouts
2 medium sized onions, sliced thin
1 can mushrooms
1 can bamboo shoots, sliced thin
2 large tomatoes, cut in 8 sections
1 cup celery, sliced diagonally in 1½ inch pieces

Sukiyaki
Japan

Heat oil in a heavy iron or aluminum frying pan. Fry 1/3 of the meat slightly then add 2 tablespoons sugar. Three minutes later add ½ cup soy sauce, cook 3 minutes, then add 1/3 of the onion. When the onion is soft, add 1/3 of the celery, mushrooms and bamboo shoots, ½ cup water or mushroom stock, and cook 3 minutes. Add 1/3 of the tomatoes, green vegetables, green onions, and bean sprouts. Add 1/3 cup more soy sauce, more sugar and water, if necessary.

The Japanese custom is to prepare sukiyaki in a frying pan over a charcoal brazier at the table. Approximately 1/3 of the ingredients are cooked in the beginning and more added as the individual bowls are filled from the frying pan. Serve hot with rice. Makes 6 servings.

---

12 frankfurters
12 wooden skewers
½ cup flour
½ teaspoon sage
½ cup cornmeal
1 teaspoon salt
2 teaspoons sugar
1 tablespoon baking powder
1 cup milk
2 eggs

Corn Dogs
United States

Insert skewer in end of each frankfurter. Steam for 7 minutes. Cool. Sift dry ingredients together. Beat milk and eggs together and blend well into dry ingredients. Dip franks in batter and fry in deep fat at 350° F. until brown. Wrap handle in paper napkin. Serve at once.

---

3 cups flour
1¼ cups mayonnaise
Juice of ½ orange or ¼ to ½ cup water

Mix ingredients and roll out to ⅛ inch thickness. Cut in rounds.

Put following ingredients on 1 round of pastry in order given:

2 small raw potatoes, sliced thin
2 small raw turnips, sliced thin
1 medium onion, sliced thin

Meat Pie
German

Top with patty of pork and beef:

1 pound ground beef to
½ pound pork, ground

Mix beef and pork and place on top of vegetable slices. Dot with butter. Moisten edge of pastry and place another round on top. Pinch edges together and bake in a 400° oven for 1 hour.

Place chicken breast (skin side down) in baking pan.

Sprinkle with:

½ teaspoon dry mustard	½ teaspoon dried sage
½ teaspoon onion powder	½ teaspoon dried oregano
½ teaspoon dried basil	

Dot with butter - ¼ cup

"Coq Au Vin"
French

Add 1 cup water and 1 cup good sherry wine. Cover and bake in 350 degree oven for 2 hours. Remove cover and allow chicken to brown.

Drain juice from chicken and thicken with cornstarch. Add ¼ cup red wine and 1 small can sliced mushrooms. Correct seasoning and serve with:

orange rice

Rice cooked in half water and half orange juice. This is grand. Season with salt, pepper and plenty of butter.

Allow ⅛ pound meat per person. Marinate venison in marinade for 48 hours. To prepare marinade cook together for 30 minutes and cool:

2 cups water	2 carrots, sliced
1 cup vinegar	½ cup sliced celery
1 onion, sliced	1 teaspoon whole peppercorns
2 parsnips, cubed	

Saddle of Venison
Europe

Marinate venison. Turn several times during the 48 hours.

Drain and dry venison. Place in roasting pan. Top with 4 slices bacon. Roast in 350 degree oven until brown. Baste with marinade as it browns. Now pour marinade and vegetables over meat, cover and roast until done, 3 to 4 hours. Lift meat to serving platter. Add 1 cup sour cream and 1 tablespoon sugar to juices; thicken with cornstarch or flour. Pour over venison and serve with favorite vegetables.

---

1 Pork Tenderloin
  (Rub with salt, pepper and oregano)

Saute:

| ½ cup chopped onions | 2 chopped bell peppers |
| 2 cloves garlic | 6 tablespoons oil |

Add:

½ cup honey	1 teaspoon dried oregano
½ cup tomato puree	1½ teaspoons salt
½ cup wine vinegar	Dash of cayenne pepper

Roast Pork
Caribbean

Pour over roast and bake covered, basting frequently. Serve with boiled onions and green rice (rice to which lots of butter and fresh chopped parsley has been added).

Tempura (Fried Shrimp or Oysters)
Japan

Batter

2/3 cup flour	2/3 cup water
¼ teaspoon salt	1 egg white beaten stiffly
2 tablespoons oil	

Combine flour, salt, oil and water. Fold in egg white. Dry shrimp or oysters. Dip in batter and fry. These are puffy and crisp.

25 large oysters
½ cup oyster liquor
½ cup cream
½ cup chopped mushrooms
1 cup chopped veal (cooked)
2 tablespoons flour

2 tablespoons butter
½ teaspoon onion juice
Salt and pepper to taste
2 egg yolks
1 tablespoon chopped parsley

Oysters Kromeskies
Old New York favorite

Scald oysters and grind up. Make sauce using melted butter and stir in the flour. Add oyster liquor, cream, mushrooms, onion juice and seasonings. Stir until thick. Add oysters and veal. Thicken a little more if not real stiff. Beat in egg yolks and parsley. Set aside to cool. Make long finger rolls. Dip in egg yolk and cracker meal. Fry until brown and serve with tomato catsup, horseradish and plenty of lemon.

---

1 - 7¾ ounce can shad roe
  (caviar is good too!)
½ cup cold water
2 tablespoons gelatin
1 - 10½ ounce can consomme

¾ cup water or fresh celery juice
1 teaspoon salt
2 teaspoons lemon juice
½ cup mayonnaise
(1 quart ring mold)

Shad Roe Mold
Europe

Drain shad roe. Separate the tiny eggs with a fork. Pour ½ cup cold water in large bowl and sprinkle gelatin on top. Let stand. Combine consomme, celery juice and salt and bring to a boil. Pour over soaked gelatin, stirring well, and cool. Add lemon juice and mayonnaise. Fold in shad roe and spoon into mold. Let stand until firm in refrigerator. Unmold and serve with tomato wedges and cold sliced cucumbers.

---

6 slices day old bread (trimmed
  and buttered)
2 cups rich milk
2 cups grated Cheddar cheese

4 whole eggs
1 teaspoon onion salt
¼ cup chopped pimento

Cheese Souffle
Southern

Place bread in 3-quart baking dish. Combine rest of ingredients. Pour over bread. Allow to stand 30 minutes until bread soaks up milk mixture. Bake in 350 degree oven 35-45 minutes or until puffy and done.

---

1 young duck
Salt and pepper
4 oranges, sliced thin with rind
1 cup orange juice

3 tablespoons Cognac
3 tablespoons Cointreau
Salt & pepper to taste again

Duckling A L'Orange
French

Place duck in roasting pan. Sprinkle with salt and pepper. Cover with orange juice and orange slices. Bake in a 350 degree oven for 2½ to 3 hours. Remove juices. Add salt and pepper to taste. Stir in Cognac and Cointreau. Thicken gravy and pour over duck. Sprinkle with Cognac and flame!

5 pounds round steak or pot roast
1 tablespoon salt
½ teaspoon pepper
2 onions, sliced
1 carrot, sliced
1 stalk celery, chopped
4 cloves
4 peppercorns
1 pint red wine vinegar
2 bay leaves
2 tablespoons kidney fat or shortening
6 tablespoons butter (if meat is not fat)
5 tablespoons flour
1 tablespoon sugar
8 gingersnaps, crushed
Potato dumplings

Pot Roast with Potato Dumplings
German

Salt and pepper meat. Combine onions, carrots, celery, cloves, peppercorns, wine vinegar, bay leaves and pour over meat. Cover and let stand in refrigerator for 4 days. On 5th day drain meat, reserving marinade liquid and saute in kidney fat until browned on all sides. Add marinade liquid. Put butter in sauce pan and melt. Add flour and stir until smooth. Add sugar and cook slowly until a nice dark brown. Add to meat. Simmer about 4 hours until meat is done. Remove from pan to platter. Stir crushed gingersnaps into juices and cook until thick. Pour over meat and potato dumplings.

POTATO DUMPLINGS:
5 cups mashed potatoes
1 egg
1 cup flour (about)
1 teaspoon salt
¼ teaspoon pepper (white)
⅛ teaspoon nutmeg

Combine potatoes, eggs, salt, pepper and nutmeg and mix thoroughly. Then add enough flour to make a workable dough. Roll out, cut and drop in boiling broth. Cook covered until done.

---

1 lb. rice
1/2 lb. pork spareribs
1 chicken, cut in pieces
1 cup shrimp
1 cup peas, cooked
1 can mussels
1 can or 1/2 cup pimentos
4 cups tomatoes
1 teaspoon garlic, minced
1 bell pepper
2 onions
1 cup olive oil
1 quart water
Salt to taste
Dash of saffron

Paella
Spain

Fry chicken, spareribs and saffron lightly in oil. Add seasonings, tomatoes, garlic, pepper and onions. You can puree these. I like them in pieces. Let cook until meat is tender about 45 minutes to 1 hour. Add rice, water and salt. When rice is almost cooked, add sweet pimentos, peas, shrimp and mussels. Cook very slowly until rice is done. Mixture should be dry with each grain of rice fluffy. You may need to add a little more water. Do not stir! Cook in earthenware if possible.

Beef Steak
Cuba

8 pieces beef, ½ inch thick
Lemon juice
Crushed garlic
Salt and pepper to taste

Pound meat until flat. Marinate in sauce made from lemon juice, garlic, salt and pepper for 1 hour. Fry until brown.

1 pound navy beans
½ pound fat salt pork
1 teaspoon salt
1 large onion
1½ tablespoons brown sugar
½ cup molasses
½ teaspoon dry mustard
Boiling water

Soak beans overnight. Drain, cover with freshly boiling water and simmer for 30 minutes. Drain. Turn into bean pot. Score fat and press into beans, leaving ¼ inch above beans. Add salt, sugar, molasses and mustard. Add scalding water to cover. Cover and bake in a slow pre-heated oven at 350° for 3 hours, without stirring, adding water as necessary to keep beans covered. Uncover during last ½ hour to brown.

BARBE Q SAUCE:
1½ pounds roasted pork
1 medium sized onion
1 teaspoon salt
1 teaspoon chili powder
¾ cup tomato catsup
½ cup hot water
1½ tablespoons Worcestershire sauce
Pinch red pepper
¼ teaspoon black pepper
1 teaspoon dry mustard

Barbe Q Baked Beans
Southern

Roast pork in slow oven at 325° uncovered until brown and tender. Pull the meat apart in bite size bits. Mince onion fine and mix all ingredients together. Place on stove and let get hot. Mix with meat. Pour over beans, mixing it through real good. Let stand overnight in refrigerator for better flavor. Reheat when you are ready to serve.

Have butcher split pigs feet. Boil in salted water for 2 hours or until tender. While still hot, dip from broth into cornmeal seasoned with salt and black pepper. Fry in bacon drippings until brown.

Fried Pigs Feet
Southern

---

1 duckling
2 teaspoons salt
¼ teaspoon ginger
⅛ teaspoon black pepper

Season duck and place in a roaster. Roast for 25 to 30 minutes per pound at 350°. Save drippings for gravy.

Roast Duckling and Wild Rice
International

WILD RICE:
1 pound wild rice
1 stalk finely minced celery
1 green pepper (minced)
1 onion (minced)
½ stick margarine
Salt and pepper
1 can mushrooms
1 can bouillon

Wash and boil wild rice according to directions on the package. Then steam until fluffy. Saute celery, pepper and onion in margarine. Add salt and pepper. When vegetables are done add mushrooms and bouillon. Pour over wild rice and serve hot.

Clean turtle. Cut up. Soak overnight in milk, salt water. Flour as for chicken and fry slowly (covered) for 1 hour. Make cream gravy. Pour over turtle.

Fried Turtle
Southern

Sausage Scrapple
Southern

½ pound pork sausage
2½ cups meat broth
1 cup cornmeal

1 teaspoon salt
¼ teaspoon pepper
1 teaspoon poultry seasoning

Cook the sausage in frying pan about 5 minutes. Drain off excess fat. Add liquid and bring to a boil. Sift in cornmeal, stirring constantly. Cook until mixture thickens. Add seasoning. Turn into loaf pan and let cool. Slice thin and fry.

Cooking Doves
Southern

1 teaspoon mustard
1 teaspoon curry powder
1 teaspoon celery salt
1 teaspoon savory salt
1 teaspoon garlic salt

2 teaspoons Worcestershire sauce
1 stick melted butter
Salt and pepper to taste
1 can mushrooms

Mix spices and seasonings with butter. Coat doves well with mixture. Bake in a 250° oven for 2 hours to 2½ hours. Make gravy with drippings and a little flour for thickening. Add a can of mushrooms to gravy. Serve over birds.

Pickled Pigs Feet or Tongue
Southern

Boil pigs feet or tongue until tender (skin tongue). Put in ½ gallon jar with 3 bay leaves, 1 large onion, sliced, 2 cloves garlic, 4 stalks celery with leaves, 1 pod red pepper. Cover with undiluted vinegar. Let stand at least for 4 hours before serving. Put pigs feet or tongue in jar while still very hot.

Sausage Casserole
Southern

1 pound pork sausage
2 tablespoons chopped parsley
1 6 oz. can tomato paste

2 cups cooked whole kernel corn
2 cups cooked lima beans
¼ cup shredded cheese

Brown sausage and parsley in a skillet over low heat. Pour off fat. Add tomato paste, corn and lima beans. Cover with cheese. Pour in casserole dish. Bake in a 350° oven until brown on top and cheese is melted.

Guinea Fowl With Juniper Berries or Wild Birds
Africa

1 cup chopped Spanish onion
1/4 cup butter, softened
2 tablespoons lemon juice
12 juniper berries, crushed
1 teaspoon dried thyme leaves
1/4 teaspoon salt

1/8 teaspoon pepper
*3 guinea hens (about 2 pounds each)
1/2 cup strained red currant or apricot preserves

1. Combine onion, 1/4 cup softened butter, the lemon juice, juniper berries, thyme, salt and pepper. Rub inside and outside of each hen with onion-butter mixture. Refrigerate covered overnight.

2. Heat oven to 425 degrees. Place hens in roasting pan. Bake, basting occasionally with pan juices, 25 to 30 minutes. Brush with preserves during last 5 minutes of roasting. Remove hens to serving platter; garnish with leaf lettuce and artichokes.

1 pound ground beef
½ pound veal, ground
½ pound pork, ground
3 eggs, beaten
24 crackers, rolled fine
½ cup milk
2 teaspoons sugar

1 tablespoon mustard
2 teaspoons celery flakes
2 tablespoons parsley
1 cup grated Romano cheese or
   Parmesan cheese
Salt to taste

Meat Balls and Tomato Sauce
Italian

Mix ingredients together and form into balls. Drop into tomato sauce and simmer for 1 hour.

---

2 No. 2½ cans tomatoes
½ cup olive oil
2 onions, chopped
2 cloves garlic, sliced
2 cans tomato paste and equal
   amount of water

¼ teaspoon oregano
2 teaspoons parsley
½ teaspoon celery salt
Pinch basil
Pinch poultry seasoning

Italian Tomato Sauce

Saute onions and garlic in olive oil. Add tomatoes and rest of ingredients. Simmer for 10 minutes. Add meat balls and simmer for 1 hour. Serve over spaghetti with Parmesan cheese.

---

2 chickens (fryers)
2 egg yolks
Bread crumbs

Parmesan cheese
Frying oil

Chicken
German Style

Dip chicken in egg yolk and mixed equal amounts of Parmesan cheese and bread crumbs. Saute in fat until brown and tender. Serve with following sauce:

SAUCE:
4 tablespoons butter
4 tablespoons flour
2 cups milk
½ cup chopped mushrooms

1 carrot sliced (boiled until
   tender)
1 onion (boiled until tender)
Bouquet of herbs
½ cup cooking sherry
2 egg yolks

Make white sauce out of flour, butter, and milk. Blend in rest of ingredients. Add sherry and beaten egg yolks just before serving.

---

1 tablespoon butter
1 small onion, minced
1 cup sweet milk
1 pound American cheese
1 can tomato soup
1 teaspoon dry mustard

1 tablespoon Worcestershire
   sauce
Salt and pepper to taste
1 can red kidney beans
1 egg, well beaten

Rinktum Ditty
Southern

Mix butter, onion, milk, cheese and soup. Add seasonings. Cook in skillet until onion is done and cheese is melted. Fold in beans and beaten egg. Cook a few minutes longer. Serve on crisp crackers.

4 tablespoons water   1 teaspoon salt
1 egg   1 cup flour (approximately)

Ravioli
Italy

Beat water, egg and salt well and add flour enough to make a dough. Knead for 3 minutes. Roll thin as paper. Cut in 4 inch squares and place 1 teaspoon of following mixture on dough.

Mixture for inside of ravioli: ½ cup cooked chopped spinach
½ cup ground beef   1 clove garlic, chopped
½ cup sausage   Salt and pepper to taste

Saute ingredients in oil and let cool. Place on ravioli squares. Press edges together. Boil in salted water 12 minutes. Serve with Italian Meat Sauce.

Oxtail Stew
German

3 oxtails, cut in 1 inch pieces   1½ cups celery
6 onions, sliced   1½ teaspoon salt
3 cups tomatoes   ¾ teaspoon pepper
3 cups carrots   Flour for thickening, if desired
3 cups turnips

Boil oxtails in water to cover for 2 hours, to 2½ hours, or until tender. Then remove oxtails from the stock and add vegetables cut in rather large pieces. Cook until tender. Replace oxtails in pan with vegetables and thicken gravy. Serve with noodles if desired.

Veal Cutlets
Southern Style

Dip cutlets in beaten egg, roll in fine cracker crumbs. Fry until golden brown in hot fat. Place in baking dish which has been buttered. Make gravy with remaining fat in skillet by adding equal amount of flour to fat. Add:

1 cup chopped tomatoes   ½ teaspoon pepper
1¼ cups water   ¼ teaspoon mustard
1½ teaspoon salt

Pour over cutlets and bake in a 400° oven for 10 minutes.

Hamburgers Cooked on Bun
Southern Style

1 pound ground round steak   ¼ teaspoon marjoram (ground)
⅛ teaspoon paprika   Dash of sage, clove, and allspice
⅛ teaspoon thyme (ground)

Mix all ingredients. Place on hamburger buns and broil until done. Slice of tomato may be broiled on hamburger if desired.

Pork Pie
Southern Style

1½ pound cubed lean pork   Salt and pepper to taste
½ bay leaf, crushed   3 tablespoons flour
1 cup sliced carrots   ¼ cup cold water
½ cup sliced celery   3 cooking apples, pared and
1 small onion   sliced thin
Hot water

Place pork, bay leaf, carrots, celery, and onion in heavy pot. Cover with hot water and simmer until pork is done. Add salt and pepper. Thicken with 3 tablespoons flour which has been mixed with ¼ cup cold water. Make alternate layers of pork mixture and sliced apples in baking dish. Top with sweet potato biscuits. Bake for 30 minutes in a 450° oven.

1 pound liver
1 medium onion
2 eggs
½ teaspoon salt
⅛ teaspoon pepper
1 tablespoon chopped parsley
1 tablespoon chopped celery
  leaves
1 tablespoon chopped green
  pepper
1 cup cooked rice
1½ cups sweet milk
½ cup bread crumbs
2 strips bacon

Liver Loaf
Denmark

Scald liver in boiling water for 10 minutes. Grind liver, onion, parsley, celery, and green pepper through food chopper. Add rest of ingredients except bacon. Turn into 2 quart baking dish or bread pan which has been well greased. Top with sliced bacon and bake for 1½ hours in a 350° oven.

---

2 small kidneys (beef)
Flour
¾ pound cubed beef steak
½ cup suet or fat
1 large onion, chopped
Hot water
1 bay leaf
3 tablespoons parsley
3 tablespoons celery tops
Salt and pepper
1 cup mushrooms
1 cup diced carrots
Rich biscuit dough

Steak and Kidney Pie
English

Soak kidneys in salt water overnight. Cut steak and kidneys in 2 inch squares and dredge with flour. Brown steak, kidney and chopped onion in suet. Add hot water to cover. Add bay leaf, parsley, celery, salt, pepper, mushrooms, carrots and simmer gently for 1 hour. Pour into a deep baking dish and top with rich pastry rolled thin. Bake in a 400° oven until crust is brown.

---

2 pounds scallops
2 tablespoons shallots
½ teaspoon salt
¼ teaspoon black pepper
½ cup dry vermouth
2 cups thick white cream sauce
Chopped fresh parsley

Coquille Saint Jacques (Sea Scallops)
French

Simmer scallops in vermouth with the shallots for about 4 minutes. Remove from juice (scallops must not be over cooked.) Blend scallop broth with white sauce. Stir in scallops. Put in sea shells. Run in hot oven to brown. Serve with chopped fresh parsley.

1/3 cup oil
1 clove garlic, minced
Juice of 4 lemons
1 1/2 teaspoon salt
1/4 teaspoon pepper
1 teaspoon curry powder
1/4 cup chopped parsley
2 1/2 lbs. sea bass or white fish,
  sliced and boned
1 lemon, sliced

Soyadia
(Chilled Spiced Fish)
Egypt

Heat the oil and cook the garlic in it for 5 minutes. Stir in the lemon juice, salt pepper, curry powder, and parsley. Heat for 2 to 3 minutes. Arrange the boned fish in a 2 quart baking dish. Pour the oil mixture over all. Cover with hot water. Cover baking dish and bake in 325 degree oven for 30 minutes. Remove cover for last 10 minutes of cooking. Chill and serve with lemon, parsley and mint.

1 pound thinly sliced veal	8 ounces dry white wine
2 tablespoons butter	½ cup thick sweet cream
2 tablespoons oil	1 teaspoon chopped fresh parsley
2 tablespoons shallots	Lemon juice
2 ounces fresh sliced mushrooms	Salt and pepper to taste

Sliced Veal with Potatoes
Austria

Saute meat quickly in butter and oil. Set aside. Add other ingredients and cook over low heat until reduced to half amount. Pour over meat and garnish with chopped parsley. Serve with potatoes (Roesti).

Potatoes (Roesti)

Boil about 8 to 10 medium sized potatoes in their skins until tender. Drain and peel immediately. Cool over night. Next day cut into thin slices. Heat about 2 heaping tablespoons each of butter and Crisco in pan. Season potatoes with salt and pepper. Fry over fire, turning them to brown and crisp all over. Lower heat and press potatoes firmly into the pan. Fry on low heat until a golden crust forms underneath. Turn out onto serving platter and serve with veal and sauce.

½ cup oil	1 tablespoon minced garlic
¼ cup parsley	1 stalk celery
2 cups chopped tomatoes	1 small green bell pepper, chopped
2 cans tomato puree	½ teaspoon basil
Salt and pepper	2 cups red wine

Cioppino
Spain

Mix all ingredients except seafoods. Simmer 1 hour. 15 minutes before serving add seafoods. When done thicken with water and cornstarch.

24 clams in shell	1 pound flounder
½ pound shrimp	½ pound crab
½ pound oysters	½ pound lobster
½ pound scallops	

2 pounds fresh fish, boned (I like haddock)	1 cup light cream
1 cup butter, cold	2 teaspoons salt
4 eggs, separated	½ teaspoon white pepper
¼ cup flour	⅛ teaspoon nutmeg
1½ teaspoon cornstarch	1 cup whipping cream
	Cracker crumbs

Fish Mousse
Denmark

Clean fish and grind through food chopper with cold butter, using fine blade. Beat in egg yolks, flour and cornstarch. Add cream gradually. Stir in salt, pepper and nutmeg. Beat egg whites until stiff. Whip cream. Fold egg whites and cream into batter. Pour batter into greased 9-inch tube cake pan or mold, which has been lightly greased, and lined with cracker crumbs. Place in shallow pan of boiling water. Bake at 325 degrees for 1 hour. Let stand a few minutes, then unmold on platter. Serve with a crisp salad.

6 slices bread (broken in pieces and and sprinkled with garlic oil)	1 teaspoon seasoned salt
	1 teaspoon onion powder
3 eggs, separated	12 ounces crab meat (precooked)
2 teaspoons Worcestershire	Black pepper to taste

Crab Maryland
New England

Beat egg yolks until light with rest of ingredients. Fold in crab meat and bread bits. Beat egg whites until stiff. Fold into crab mixture. Fry like omelet in butter. Fold over and serve immediately.

½ cup chopped shallots
1 teaspoon minced garlic
4 tablespoons butter
1 teaspoon thyme
1 teaspoon basil
1 cup sauterne
¼ cup sherry

1 tablespoon Dijon mustard
Salt and pepper to taste
2 pounds boiled shrimp
Cornstarch and water to thicken
1 cup cracker crumbs
Butter

Shrimp Dijon
French

Saute shallots and garlic in butter for 5 minutes. Add thyme, basil, wines, mustard, salt and pepper. Bring to a boil and thicken with cornstarch and water. Stir in shrimp. Put in casserole and top with crumbs. Dot with butter and bake in 350 degree oven until brown, about 20 minutes.

---

1 can mushrooms
½ cup butter
4 tablespoons minced parsley
½ cup sherry

½ teaspoon mustard
½ teaspoon paprika
2 cups white sauce, thick

Lobster Thermidor
Southern

Have butcher cut 4 lobsters lengthwise. Saute lobsters in butter with mushrooms about 2 minutes. Then add mustard, paprika, parsley and sherry. Mix in cream sauce and return lobster mixture to shells. Sprinkle with cracker crumbs and butter. Brown in oven.

MEAT BALLS:
½ pound lean beef
¼ pound veal
¼ pound pork
1 cup bread crumbs
2 diced garlic cloves

½ cup grated cheese, Italian
1 tablespoon finely chopped parsley
1 egg, beaten
Salt and pepper to taste

La Sagna
Italian

Knead ingredients thoroughly together and shape into meat balls. Brown in ½ cup olive oil or bacon fat in skillet. Transfer to saucepan. Add one large can of tomatoes and simmer about 2 hours. To skillet containing juices of meat balls add 2 cloves of garlic and 1 chopped medium onion. Saute very slowly with lid on until these ingredients are thoroughly cooked. Remove onions and garlic and add to juices in the skillet 1 can of tomato paste. Saute paste until very loose. Add contents of entire skillet to the saucepan containing meat balls. Medium green pepper or mushrooms may be added if desired.

Bake or roast 1 small chicken. Cook and strip. Saute 1 pound lean pork. Remove and cut into small pieces. Pour La Sagna macaroni or heavy noodle type macaroni into pot of boiling water. Strain when done and pour into oiled deep pyrex baking dish. Add grated Mozzarello cheese, stripped chicken, pork, meat balls, sauce and ricotta. Cottage cheese (creamed) will substitute for ricotta if necessary. Repeat this procedure for the second layer. Place in a 300° oven and bake for ½ hour or until La Sagna has been bubbling for about 10 minutes. NOTE: 1 pound ground meat makes 8 good sized meat balls.

8 hard cooked eggs, diced
3 cups rich cream sauce
¾ pound crisp cooked, crumbled

½ teaspoon curry powder
½ teaspoon Worcestershire sauce

Egg Souffle
Southern

Salt and pepper to taste
    bacon

Add curry powder, Worcestershire sauce, salt and pepper to white sauce. Make alternate layers of eggs, sauce and bacon in a 3-quart baking dish. End up with bacon and brown in 350 degree oven for 20-30 minutes.

---

4 tablespoons butter
4 tablespoons flour
2 cups cream or milk
1 pint oysters

Cracker crumbs (Saltines)
Salt and black pepper
½ stick butter

Scalloped Oysters
Southern

Make white sauce. Stir in oysters, salt and pepper to taste. Make layers of oyster sauce - cracker crumbs - ending up with cracker crumbs. Dot with butter. Bake in 375 degree oven for 20 minutes or until hot and bubbly.

½ cup lard
2 pounds veal
2 small onions
2 tomatoes

2 sweet peppers
1 cup water
Salt and pepper to taste
Flour

Veal
Spanish

Brown veal in skillet in lard. Remove browned veal. Saute onions, tomatoes and peppers. Add water. Sprinkle with flour, salt and pepper. Return veal to mixture. Cover and let simmer until tender.

3-5 pounds pork
½ teaspoon salt
¼ teaspoon pepper

2 cups boiling water
4 tablespoons flour

Roast Pork
Southern

Score fat side of pork. Brush with salt and pepper. Place fat side up in roaster. Cook in a 325° oven, allowing 40 minutes per pound. When done add 2 cups boiling water to drippings. Thicken gravy with 4 tablespoons flour.

---

4 teaspoons oil
½ cup diced onion
1½ pounds diced meat
3 tablespoons cornstarch

¾ teaspoon salt
⅛ teaspoon pepper
2 tablespoons soy sauce
1 can Chinese vegetables

Chop Suey
Chinese

Saute onions and meat in oil. Add rest of ingredients. Simmer about 10 minutes and serve on rice.

1½ pound beef   ½ pound pork

Mix meat (ground well). Season with salt and pepper. Make into ¾ inch patties. Fry in hot fat until brown on both sides. Add 1 can mushrooms and 1 cup coffee. Steam until done.

Beef
Hungarian Style

---

8 veal chops	4 tablespoons catsup
4 cloves garlic	2 tablespoons vinegar
⅔ cup salad oil	½ teaspoon black pepper
6 tablespoons soy sauce	

Mix garlic, oil, soy sauce, catsup, vinegar and black pepper. Marinate chops in mixture for 2 hours. Broil until tender, placing about 6 inches from top of burner.

Broiled Veal Chops Pacific
Australian

---

3 to 4 pound chuck roast	1 cup canned tomatoes
Salt and pepper	2 onions, sliced
Prepared mustard	1 yellow turnip
Flour	1 acorn squash
1 tablespoon drippings	

Rub roast with salt and pepper, spread with mustard and flour well all over. Place in roasting pan and brown on top of stove with drippings. Slice onions, turnip and squash and place around roast. Do not slice too small. Season with salt. Then add tomatoes and bake covered for about 3 hours in a 350° oven.

Old-Fashioned Pot Roast
Southern

---

8 pork chops	1 tablespoon chopped parsley
½ pound sausage	1 small onion, grated
2 cups minute rice, cooked	1 teaspoon poultry seasoning
1 tablespoon chopped celery	½ teaspoon salt
leaves	⅛ teaspoon pepper
1 tablespoon sausage drippings	

Have butcher cut pockets in pork chops. Mix rest of ingredients and stuff pork chops. Bake for 1½ to 2 hours in a 350° oven, covered. Brown before serving by removing top.

Pork Chops with Sausage Stuffling
Southern

Boil tongue for 1½ hours with the following seasonings:

2 bay leaves   1 teaspoon thyme
½ teaspoon cloves

When done skin. Let Cool. Dip in egg or cracker crumbs and fry until brown.

Fried Tongue
Southern

Stuffed Ham
Southern

12-14 pound ham
1 quart water
2 cups cracker crumbs
2 large onions, chopped
2 teaspoons thyme
2 teaspoons cloves

1 teaspoon allspice
1 teaspoon celery seed
1 teaspoon powdered ginger
1 teaspoon dry mustard
1 teaspoon Worcestershire
  sauce

Place ham in covered roaster on top of the stove with water. Let simmer for about an hour. Remove from stove. Let cool. Mix bread crumbs, onion and rest of seasonings together with enough juice from ham to moisten. Stuff by taking wooden spoon and making holes, going as deep as possible. Cover top of ham with more stuffing. Put in a 350° oven for about 2 hours. If any stuffing is left make patties.

Spetinis
Italian

2 veal cutlets
Garlic
1 cup Wesson or olive oil

Juice of 1 lemon
Salt and pepper to taste
Bay leaf

Pound cutlets very thin. Cut in strips. Rub each piece with garlic, salt and pepper. Mix oil and lemon juice. Dip meat strips in oil mixture, sprinkle with Parmesan cheese and roll each steak like jelly roll. Stick skewer through meat adding a bay leaf between each spetini. Broil for 20 to 25 minutes turning once and basting with remaining oil and lemon juice.

Broiled Ground Round Steak
International

1 pound beef, ground
1 tablespoon onion, ground
1 clove garlic, minced
1 teaspoon thick tomato paste

½ teaspoon dill pickle, minced
½ teaspoon mustard
½ teaspoon Worcestershire
  sauce

Mix all ingredients together. Broil in hot oven until desired doneness. Makes 6 patties.

Pizza
Italian

1 package yeast
1 tablespoon water
1½ teaspoons sugar
1½ teaspoons salt

½ cup shortening, melted
2 cups boiling water
Approximately 6 cups flour

Make yeast dough. Let rise for 1½ hours. Roll dough thin and spread the following ingredients on big round of dough (¼ inch thick). Do not let dough rise before baking. The thinner the dough the crisper your Pizza will be.

SPREAD FOR DOUGH:
1. Mozzerella cheese or Italian cheese
2. Tomato sauce (sparingly)
3. Dot with chunks of canned tomato
4. Sprinkle with garlic salt
5. Sprinkle with oregano
6. Dot with piece of sausage, green olives or anchovies
7. Sprinkle with Parmesan cheese
8. Sprinkle with anise seed

Bake in a 450° oven for approximately 15 minutes.

2 pounds round steak
1 cup flour
3 tablespoons fat
1 onion, sliced

1 No. 2 can tomatoes
2 teaspoons salt
½ teaspoon pepper

Swiss Steak
International

Pound flour into steak on both sides. Melt fat in skillet. Brown well on both sides. Place in baking dish. Add onions and tomatoes. Add enough water to cover meat. Cover with tight lid and bake in a 325° oven for 2½ hours. Salt and pepper to taste.

---

6 pork chops
1 package lima beans
1 No. 2 can tomatoes
1 small green pepper
1 medium onion

1 teaspoon sugar
1 teaspoon salt
Dash of pepper
Pinch of thyme

Pork Chop Casserole
Southern

Brown pork chops. Mix all other ingredients. Place in a casserole dish. Top with pork chops and bake in oven for 35 minutes.

---

2 tablespoons kitchen fat, melted
3 tablespoons flour
2 teaspoons salt
Pepper
1 teaspoon chili powder
⅛ teaspoon dry mustard

1 bay leaf
Dash of curry
Dash of sage
3 cups canned tomatoes
1 8 oz. package macaroni
8 to 10 wieners

Macaroni-Wiener Medley
Southern

In skillet heat fat. Add flour then tomatoes, stirring constantly. Add spices. Stir until thick. Place wieners on top of sauce. Cover with tight fitting lid and steam for 10 to 15 minutes. Serve over cooked macaroni.

---

1 lamb chop, veal, pork or steak
¼ large onion
½ tomato
½ green pepper

¼ small eggplant
Garlic salt to taste
Basil
Pepper and salt to taste

Lamb or Chops in Foil
Southern

Arrange vegetables on foil. Lay chops on top of the vegetables. Sprinkle with seasonings. Wrap all up securely in foil. Bake for 1 hour at 350°. Serves 1.

½ cup vinegar
2 tablespoons Worcestershire sauce
2 tablespoons tomato catsup

¼ pound butter
Red hot sauce to taste
Salt and pepper each piece chicken

Barbe-Q-Chicken
Southern

For 1 chicken (frying or broiler size) baste with the following sauce and bake for 1 hour in a 350° oven.

Goulash
Hungarian

1 pound veal loin, cubed	1½ teaspoon salt
1 pound lamb shoulder, cubed	½ teaspoon pepper
1 pound fresh pork, cubed	½ teaspoon paprika
2 small onions	1 cup water
2 tablespoons margarine	1 cup bouillon
2 tablespoons flour	Hot cooked noodles

Slice onions. Heat butter in deep pot and saute onions until transparent. Add meat and cook for 10 minutes. Sprinkle with flour and stir. Add seasonings, water and bouillon. Increase water if necessary to cover meat. Cover pot. Bring to a boil and boil for 5 minutes. Lower heat and let cook slowly for 1½ hours or until meat is tender and liquid has cooked down to a thick sauce. Serve over hot noodles.

Spice Round
Tennessee

10 to 12 pound round of beef	½ tablespoon cayenne pepper
½ teaspoon saltpeter	1 tablespoon ginger
2 cups brown sugar	1 tablespoon ground cinnamon
2 cups salt	1 tablespoon allspice
3 tablespoons chopped onion	1 tablespoon nutmeg
3 pounds beef suet	2 tablespoons black pepper

Mix saltpeter, sugar and salt. Rub into each side of meat. Let stand one night in a cool place. Wipe off. Grind onion and suet. Add seasonings. Make holes in beef and stuff with spiced mixture. Let stand for 2 weeks. Boil spice round 20 minutes to the pound. Let cool and slice.

Enchiladas
Mexico

TORTILLAS:

1 cup flour	2 cups milk
½ cup corn meal, white	3 eggs, beaten
½ teaspoon salt	1 teaspoon baking powder

Beat eggs until light; add milk and salt. Sift together flour, meal and baking powder. Add to egg mixture and beat until smooth. Bake on hot griddle in about 5 inch circle, until light brown, turning once. Spread with enchilada filling, roll up and sprinkle with cheese and bake for 20 minutes in a 375° oven. Serve hot.

ENCHILADA FILLING:

⅓ cup olive oil	Salt and pepper
1 pound ground steak	2 cans stewed tomatoes
½ pound ground pork	1 teaspoon chili powder
4 medium onions, diced	1 pound American cheese

Saute onions in olive oil. Add meat, tomatoes, and seasonings. Cook until thick, about 40 minutes. Spread on tortillas, sprinkle with cheese and bake.

Chicken Burgers
Southern

2 cups ground uncooked chicken	1½ teaspoon salt
1 cup thin cream	1⅛ teaspoon nutmeg
	½ cup bread crumbs

Mix all ingredients and shape into patties. Broil about 7 minutes on each side.

8 veal cutlets
English mustard
Worcestershire sauce
Salt and pepper

Flour
Beaten egg
Cracker crumbs

Wiener Schnitzel
German

Rub mustard on veal cutlets. Sprinkle with Worcestershire sauce. Sprinkle with salt and pepper. Dip in flour, beaten egg and then cracker crumbs. Fry in skillet until tender.

Prepare veal as for Schnitzel. Cover with crab, asparagus tips and sauce Bernaise. Run under boiler until hot and bubbly. Serve with a slice of crisp bacon and watercress.

Veal Oscar
United States

Prepare Schnitzel and cover with sour cream and fresh sliced mushroom. Broil until bubbly.

Yager Schnitzel
German

---

2 to 3 pounds lamb, cubed
2 tablespoons fat
2 tablespoons chopped parsley
3 tablespoons chopped celery
  leaves
1 tablespoon salt
Dash of pepper

½ cup pearl barley
2 quarts water
8 small onions
4 potatoes
6 carrots
1 No. 2½ can green beans

Hot Scotch Pot
Scotland

Saute lamb, parsley, celery leaves in fat until brown. Put in large pot with rest of ingredients and simmer for approximately 1½ hours. Vegetables may be added the last 30 minutes if you prefer they not be cooked to a mush.

---

1 pound frankfurters
⅓ cup chopped onions
2 tablespoons fat
¾ cup water

¾ cup tomato catsup
2 tablespoons brown sugar
½ teaspoon dry mustard
1 can sour kraut

Franks and Kraut Casserole
Southern

Saute onions in fat. Add water, catsup, brown sugar and mustard. Heat thoroughly. Put kraut in casserole. Place franks on kraut. Cover with sauce. Bake for 30 minutes in a 375° oven.

---

3 pounds shrimp
1 quart water
1 cup vinegar
1½ teaspoons caraway seed
1½ teaspoon pickling spice
1½ teaspoons whole peppercorns

⅛ teaspoon salt
1 bay leaf
½ teaspoon dry mustard
½ teaspoon red pepper
Handful celery leaves

Spiced Shrimp
International

Mix water, vinegar and spices. Simmer for 20 minutes. Then add shrimp and boil for 10 minutes or until done. Remove from water and let each person shell their own shrimp.

Calves Brains and Scrambled Eggs
Southern

1 pound brains (calves)
5 eggs
4 tablespoons bacon drippings
Water
Salt and pepper to taste

Remove membrane from brains. Place in skillet with bacon drippings and water to cover. Simmer until dry. Scramble eggs in brains and season with salt and pepper.

Chicken Tetrazzini
Italy

1-2 pound fryer (boned)
½ pound broiled mushrooms
Plenty of butter
Freshly grated Parmesan cheese
Spaghetti
Evaporated milk
Salt and pepper to taste

Saute mushrooms in butter. Add pepper. Add chicken and cover with evaporated milk. Let simmer over low flame for 10 minutes. Cook ¼ pound spaghetti. Place in baking dish and sprinkle with cheese and butter. Pour in chicken mixture. Add more milk if needed. Bake in a 315° oven for 15 minutes.

Batter Fried Chicken
Southern

Dip chicken in following batter and fry in fat slowly.

BATTER:
1½ cups flour
1 tablespoon baking powder
½ teaspoon salt
1 egg, well beaten
½ cup milk

Mix and sift dry ingredients. Mix egg and milk and combine with dry ingredients. Dip each piece of chicken in batter and fry in deep fat until brown. Cook chicken until tender.

Poached Salmon in Court Bouillon
French

1 whole Salmon (4-5 lbs)
Make Court Bouillon with
3 quarts water
1/2 cup white vinegar or lemon juice
3 minced carrots
2 onions minced
1 rib celery minced
1/4 cup minced parsley
1 tablespoon coarse salt
1 teaspoon dried thyme
1 bay leaf
1 lb. peppercorn added last 15 min
Simmer 1 hour

Add Salmon to simmered broth and simmer covered for 20 minutes. Skin Salmon and serve with lemon butter

Cold Glazed Salmon
Denmark

Salmon is grand served hot with lemon butter, chives and cracked pepper.
But my favorite way is to glaze it!

Glaze

1 envelope of plain gelatin
2 cups of fish broth (hot)

Mix gelatin first with a little cold water. Then melt in hot broth. Allow to cool until it starts to set. Spoon over salmon which you have placed on a serving platter. Sprinkle lightly with paprika. Chill in refrigerator.

1 goose
1 clove garlic
2 teaspoons olive oil
½ cup chopped onion
¼ cup chopped celery

½ teaspoon cinnamon
2 anise seeds
¾ cup soy sauce
1 tablespoon sugar
2 cups hot water

Roast Goose
Chinese

Mix all ingredients together and fill cavity of goose. Sew or skewer together so juice cannot run out. Place in roaster and bake at 350° until tender, basting frequently with the following mixture:

2 cups boiling water, ½ cup honey, ¼ cup vinegar and 1 tablespoon soy sauce.

Goose should roast tender in about 3½ hours. Drain liquid from goose and thicken for gravy with cornstarch.

---

2 pimientoes
5 tablespoons green pepper
6 ripe olives
3 tablespoons butter
1 teaspoon salt

¼ teaspoon pepper
Dash cayenne
1 can mushroom soup
1 can salmon
Recipe biscuits

Salmon Pie
Southern

Saute pimientoes, pepper, olives in butter. Add salt, pepper and cayenne to soup. Remove oil from salmon. Add to sauteed ingredients and then add to soup. Pull each biscuit out to ⅛ inch. Line muffin tins with biscuit. Fill with salmon mixture and bake for 30 minutes at 400°

Wrap turkey in a well greased muslin cloth. Place in large roaster with sufficient water to make gravy if desired. Bake in a 300° oven allowing approximately 30 minutes per pound. Reserve juice for gravy and dressing.

Turkey and Cornbread Dressing
Southern

4 cups cornbread
2 cups left over cold biscuit or
  bread
⅓ cup ground onion
1 cup ground celery
2 tablespoons chopped parsley
1½ teaspoons salt

1 teaspoon poultry seasoning
1 teaspoon sage
½ teaspoon pepper
Turkey juice to moisten well
4 tablespoons melted butter (if
  turkey is not fat)

Mix all ingredients thoroughly. Bake in large baking pan for 1 hour in a 375° oven or until well browned.

---

2 chickens (2 pounds each)
½ cup olive oil
3½ cups canned tomatoes
1 onion, sliced
2 cloves garlic

3 tablespoons chopped parsley
Pinch salt, thyme and pepper
½ cup cooking sauterne
1 small can chopped ripe olives

Chicken Cacciatore
Italian

Saute chicken in olive oil until tender. Add tomatoes, onion, garlic, parsley and seasonings. Cook for 30 minutes. Just before serving stir in sauterne and ripe olives.

1 can oysters   1 can crab meat
1 can salmon   1 can tuna

Drain seafood and reserve the liquid to make sauce.

Seafood Casserole
Southern

WHITE SAUCE:
6 tablespoons butter   milk if necessary.
6 tablespoons flour   Black pepper to taste
2 cups liquid from seafood and Salt to taste

Melt butter in saucepan. Add flour. Stir until smooth then add liquid and cook until thick. Place mixed seafood in casserole. Top with sauce, cracker crumbs and dot with butter. Brown in hot oven until hot through.

Omelet   1 can tomato paste
                                2 cans mushrooms (small)
SAUCE: 1 tablespoon Worcestershire
2 tablespoons butter   sauce
6 onions   Salt and pepper
1 green pepper   1 tablespoon minced parsley

Omelet
Spanish Style

Saute all ingredients until tender. Pour over omelet made with 6 eggs and 6 tablespoons cream.

---

1 medium onion, minced   1 can tuna
½ green pepper, minced   2 eggs
2 tablespoon olive oil   Salt and pepper to taste
1 large egg plant   Bread or cracker crumbs
½ cup cream   Butter

Egg Plant and Tuna Casserole
Southern

Saute onions and pepper in olive oil. Add egg plant and about 1 cup water. Cover and steam until egg plant is tender. Add tuna, cream, beaten eggs, salt and pepper. Put in baking dish; top with crumbs, and plenty of butter. Bake for 25 minutes in a 350° oven or until brown.

---

4 eggs, separated   ¼ cup water added to the
½ teaspoon salt   whites

Omelet
French Style

Whip egg whites and water until stiff, not dry. To the egg yolks add 2 tablespoons flour and beat until light and thick. Fold beaten yolks and whites together. Handle gently. Heat 2 tablespoons fat in skillet. Pour in egg mixture. Reduce heat. Put lid on skillet and cook slowly for 5 to 8 minutes. Remove cover and continue cooking for 20 minutes until knife inserted in center comes out clean. Cut omelet and fold over.

---

6 eggs   Chopped green onions
Cream or milk   Salt and white pepper
6 tablespoons butter

Shirred Eggs
International

Cover bottom of individual baking dishes with milk. Break into dishes 1 or 2 eggs. Sprinkle with salt and pepper, chopped onions and 1 tablespoon butter. Bake in a 350° oven until firm.

3 pounds sirloin steak
3 cups soy sauce
¼ cup brown sugar

1 tablespoon ginger
1 clove garlic

Steak Teriyaki
Japanese

Marinate steak at least for 30 minutes in sauce made from soy sauce, brown sugar, ginger and garlic. Broil for 5 to 10 minutes on each side.

---

1 pint mushrooms
1½ pounds sweetbreads
3 cups stock
Salt and pepper
2 teaspoons onion juice

4 eggs
2 tablespoons flour
4 tablespoons cold water
2 teaspoons lemon juice
2 teaspoons minced parsley

Sweetbreads and Mushrooms in Egg Sauce
International

Boil sweetbreads in salted water with juice of ½ lemon added for 15 minutes. Drain. Cut in small pieces. Season stock with salt, pepper and onion juice. Beat eggs with flour and cold water and remaining lemon juice. Add to stock. Stir until thick. Add parsley, mushrooms and sweetbreads. Serve hot on toast.

---

1 young 5 pound leg of lamb
4 pods garlic
Handful of parsley
1 green pepper
1 onion
1 pint red wine

1 can mushrooms
1 can tomatoes
½ cup olive oil
Pinch of basil
1 bay leaf
Salt and pepper

Roast Leg of Lamb
Italian Style

Stab holes in lamb and stuff with parsley and garlic. Put in 500° oven. Brush top well with olive oil and roast until tender, allowing 25 minutes to the pound. Pour red wine over roast the last 30 minutes of cooking time. In the meantime, make sauce as follows: Saute chopped pepper and onion in olive oil until tender. Add tomatoes, mushrooms, basil, bay leaf, salt and pepper and simmer until reduced to ½ amount. Add drippings from lamb and thickening if desired. Serve with lamb.

2½ pounds fresh cod
3 medium onions chopped
4 or 5 medium tomatoes
½ cup rice (cooked)
1 cup apple cider

1 cup oil and butter
1 clove garlic
1 teaspoon dried parsley
Salt and pepper to taste

Cod Fish
Portugal

Divide cod into steaks. Put in deep frying pan with the oil and butter, chopped onions (previously cooked to a light golden color), finely chopped tomatoes, garlic, rice and parsley. Season with salt and pepper. Cover pan and cook for 8 minutes. Uncover pan. Add the cider and cook approximately 5 to 8 minutes more. Arrange fish on platter and cover with contents of the pan.

Shrimp and Okra Gumbo
Southern

2 pounds raw shrimp
1 pound okra
2 tablespoons shortening
⅓ cup shortening
½ cup flour
1 large onion, chopped

6 cups water
1 tablespoon vinegar
Salt, red and black pepper to taste
Filé powder

Wash and cook shrimp in boiling water with 1 tablespoon vinegar for 7 minutes. Peel shrimp. Reserve the stock. Cut okra in ¼ inch pieces. Heat 2 tablespoons shortening in skillet. Add okra and cook over medium heat until smooth. Heat 1/3 cup shortening in a pan. Add flour and cook at medium heat until a rich dark brown, stirring constantly. Add chopped onion, okra, stock and seasoning to taste. Cook slowly for 30 minutes. Add shrimp and cook for 15 minutes longer. Serve hot over rice with a dash of filé.

Fried Chicken Pie
Southern

1 chicken stewed and boned
4 tablespoons margarine
1 tablespoon chopped green onion
4 tablespoons flour
2 cups chicken stock

1 teaspoon chopped pimiento
1 teaspoon Worcestershire sauce
1 tablespoon parsley, chopped
Salt and pepper to taste
Pie crust

Saute onion in margarine until done. Add flour and blend well. Stir in chicken stock and cook until thick. Add chicken and rest of ingredients. Roll pastry into 5 inch rounds. Spoon chicken mixture out on ½ of the pastry. Fold other half over filling and seal edges with a fork. Fry in deep fat as for fruit fried pies.

Tuna Croquettes
Southern

4 cups flaked tuna
2 cups thick white sauce
2 tablespoons minced parsley
½ teaspoon salt
¼ teaspoon cayenne pepper

1 tablespoon lemon juice
Cracker crumbs
1 egg
1 tablespoon water

Combine tuna with white sauce and seasonings and chill. Form into croquettes and roll in finely crushed crackers. Dip in beaten eggs and again in crackers. If possible chill 1 hour and fry in deep fat until brown.

Baked Stuffed Fish
International

3 to 4 pound fish
Flour, salt and pepper

STUFFING:
¼ cup cracker crumbs
¼ cup stale bread crumbs

½ tablespoon melted butter
⅛ teaspoon salt
½ teaspoon onion juice
1 teaspoon chopped parsley
1 teaspoon capers or pickles

Mix all ingredients. Stuff into fish. Coat the outside of fish with flour, salt and pepper. Bake fish at 375° for 1 hour or until tender. Baste with tomato juice.

2 tablespoons butter
⅛ green pepper shredded
1 cup thinly sliced mushrooms
2 tablespoons flour
½ teaspoon salt
2 cups cream
3 cups chicken, diced (cooked)

¼ cup butter, creamed
3 egg yolks
1 teaspoon onion juice
1 tablespoon lemon juice
½ teaspoon paprika
2 tablespoons cooking sherry
Chopped pimiento

Original Chicken-a-La King
Southern

Saute green pepper and mushrooms in butter until done. Add flour, salt, cream and stir until smooth. Add chicken.

Cream butter with egg yolks, onion juice, lemon juice and paprika. Add to hot chicken mixture. Simmer slowly until thick. Just before serving add sherry and chopped pimiento.

---

1 3½ pound chicken
3 tablespoons salad oil
1 clove garlic, mashed
6 to 8 green onions
Salt and pepper

½ cup hot water
1½ cups milk
3 tablespoons flour
1 to 2 tablespoons curry powder

Curried Chicken
International

Saute chicken in fat until tender. Add garlic, green onions, salt and pepper and water. Steam until onions are done. Add flour to liquid in skillet. Add milk and curry powder. Cook until thick. Serve with rice.

---

4 pounds ribs
1 teaspoon salt
⅛ teaspoon pepper

4 slices lemon
1 large onion, chopped

Barbe-Q-Beef Ribs
Southern

Place spare ribs meaty side up in a dripping pan. Sprinkle with salt and pepper. Top with lemon slices and onion. Bake at 450° for 30 minutes uncovered.

SAUCE:
1 teaspoon chili powder
1 tablespoon celery seed
¼ cup brown sugar
¼ cup vinegar

¼ cup Worcestershire sauce
1 cup tomato catsup
2 cups water
Dash of tobasco sauce

Combine ingredients and bring to boiling point. Pour over ribs. Continue baking in a moderate over at 350° for 1 hour. Baste ribs often.

---

6 hard cooked eggs
5 finely chopped anchovies
½ cup soft bread crumbs
Pepper to taste

2½ tablespoons melted butter
Heavy cream
1 beaten egg
Bread crumbs

Fried Stuffed Eggs
Italian

Add anchovies, crumbs, pepper and butter to egg yolks and enough cream to make mixture soft enough to handle. Fill egg whites. Press halves together. Dip in beaten egg, then in bread crumbs. Cook until golden brown in deep fat. Serve with tomato sauce.

Williamsburg Chicken Surprise
Southern

1 chicken, boiled
Salt and pepper
2 tablespoons parsley
2 tablespoons onion
2 tablespoons celery
6 slices ham

DRESSING:
2 cups bread crumbs
1 minced onion
2 tablespoons parsley
½ teaspoon sage and savory
Salt and pepper
Moisten with chicken broth
White sauce (2 cups)

Boil chicken with parsley, onion and celery. Salt and pepper. When tender place in casserole dish. Make dressing out of bread and seasonings. Spread ham slices with dressing and roll up. Place in casserole with chicken. Cover with white sauce and bake in a 350° oven for 45 minutes.

Eggs Cuernavaca
Mexico

Saute eggs or poach until whites are firm. Lay in shallow dish. Pour medium white sauce over eggs. Let set until cold. Roll each egg in fine bread crumbs. Dip in beaten egg and back into bread crumbs. Saute in small amount of fat until golden brown.

Oysters Rockefeller
International

5 tablespoons butter
5 tablespoons minced cooked spinach
2 tablespoons finely minced onion
1½ tablespoons minced cooked lettuce

2 teaspoons minced celery
¼ teaspoon herb blend (for fish)
¼ teaspoon anchovy paste
Salt and pepper to taste

Saute butter with all ingredients until brown and tender. Place oysters on shells and broil slowly for 5 minutes. Cover with remaining ingredients. Sprinkle with bread crumbs, dot with butter and broil until thoroughly heated and brown.

Egg Roll
China

SKIN:
1 egg beaten and divided in half
2 cups flour
¼ cup cornstarch
Enough water to make ½ thickness of pancakes
STUFFING:
2 boiled chicken breasts

(minced)
½ pound boiled shrimp (minced)
½ head cabbage (boiled 5 minutes, drained and minced)
½ teaspoon white pepper
1 teaspoon salt
2 teaspoons shortening

Make skin by beating ½ egg, flour, cornstarch and enough water to make a thin batter. Strain batter. Cook the skin until it pops away from small skillet. Turn the skin and cook slowly on the other side. Mix all ingredients for stuffing. Place in each egg roll skin. Roll up skin. Use other ½ egg to seal edges and fry to a golden brown in hot fat.

The secret to make perfect skins for egg roll is to have small pan hot and lightly greased. Pour batter into pan and then immediately pour out batter that does not adhere to the pan. This will give a thin skin for the egg rolls.

Dough:

1/2 lb. cold salt butter or margarine
6 1/2 cups flour

3/4 to 1 cup cold water
1 teaspoon salt

Beef Filling:

1/2 cup vegetable oil
4 medium onions, peeled and
  chopped
1 1/2 lb. ground chuck
2 sweet roasted pimento, drained
  and chopped
1/2 cup dark seedless raisins

1 1/2 teaspoons oregano
1 teaspoon sweet paprika
Pinch of black pepper
1 tablespoon salt
4 large eggs, hard-cooked, peeled
  and chopped
24 small green pitted olives

Dough: Cut butter into pieces, using electric mixer, mix with flour and salt. Gradually add 3/4 cup water. Mix for 6 minutes. Dough should form a ball. Pat into round shape. Place dough in plastic bag and keep at room temperature for 20 to 30 minutes. Divide dough in half and knead for 2 minutes. Roll out on lightly floured surface to a thickness of 1/8 inch and 5 1/2 inches in diameter. Should make enough for 24 circles.

Beef Filling: Heat oil in skillet and saute onion until bright yellow. Add beef, stirring until beef loses it's red color. Stir in pimento, raisins, oregano, paprika, and salt and contiune sauteing for 2 minutes. Drain off excess oil; chill in refrigerator for 1 hour. Stir in chopped eggs just before filling the dough. Reserve olives to add to each empanada.

Preparing the Empanada: Preheat oven to 450 degrees. Place 4 tablespoons of filling on each circle of dough. Inscrt 1 olive into each mound of filling. If dough is dry, moisten with cold water. Fold dough in half. Press down firmly just below the mound of filling. Turn edge over, pressing down firmly. Then working from left to right, crimp and pleat in points to seal edges. Brush each empanada with a glaze made of 1 egg, beaten with 1/2 teaspoon sugar. Place empanadas 1 inch apart on an ungreased baking sheet and bake for 20 minutes or until golden brown. Left over baked empanadas can be stored in the refrigerator and reheated for 10 minutes at 350 degrees. Yield 24.

Empanada
Argentina

Souvlakia is popular in Greece. It is grilled meat on skewers, lamb, pork or swordfish. It is generally marinated with oil, lemon juice, parsley, salt and pepper. The meat is then skewered alternately with tomato and bay leaves and broiled for 15 minutes. It is then sprinkled with fresh oregano.

Souvlakia
Greece

---

1 Rabbit, cut up
oil (enough for saute)
water (enough to make sauce)
red wine, (Beaujolais)
pepper, to taste

1 onion chopped
1/4 cup flour
3 bay leaves
salt, to taste

Marinade rabbit with 1/3 or 1/2 bottle of red wine, salt, pepper, bay leaves, for 24 hours.

Saute rabbit in hot oil until brown. Remove pieces, set aside. In same pan saute onion until tender, add flour, then water to make sauce. Add the wine and bay leaves used for marinade, rabbit pieces; cover and simmer 1 1/2 to 2 hours.

Delicious with mashed potatoes and green beans with garlic butter and French bread.

Rabbit
(French Style)

1 1/2 to 2 pounds veal steak
1/2 pound prosciutto ham or
    smoked cooked ham
1/4 cup grated Parmesan cheese
1/2 cup bread crumbs
Few rosemary leaves

1/8 teaspoon sage
Pepper to taste
Cooking oil
1/4 pound butter
1/4 cup sherry wine

Veal Birds
Southern

Pound veal very thin and cut into pieces about 3 X 4 inches. Grind ham with cheese, bread crumbs, rosemary and sage. Season with pepper and add about 1 tablespoon oil or enough to blend stuffing into smooth mixture. Place about 1 teaspoon onto each veal piece, roll up and secure with toothpicks. Heat butter in large skillet with 1 tablespoon oil. Add veal birds and cook about 15 minutes or until fork tender, turning often to brown on all sides. Sprinkle on sherry and cook about 3 minutes more. Transfer to serving dish and pour on pan juices. Serves 4.

Eggbread:

2 cups cornmeal
1 cup buttermilk
1/2 teaspoon soda
1 teaspoon baking powder

1 teaspoon salt
6 tablespoons fat or lard
2 whole eggs

Combine all ingredients. Pour into a well-greased pan and bake in 350 degree oven for 25 minutes. Cut in squares and split. Place slices of chicken on bread and serve hot with sauce.

Chicken on Eggbread
(An old Southern treat)

Sliced Cooked Chicken

Sauce:

3 tablespoons minced onions
1/2 cup butter
3 cups chicken broth
Salt and pepper to taste

3 tablespoons minced celery
5 tablespoons flour
1/4 cup cream
Dash of nutmeg

To make sauce, saute onion and celery in butter. Stir in 5 tablespoons flour until blended. Add chicken broth. Cook (stirring constantly) until thick. Add cream and season to taste with salt, pepper, and a dash of nutmeg.

Cut chicken up and put into pan of hot water. While chicken is hot from the water, dip into flour and place into hot fat. Cover and cook 5 minutes. Remove lid and continue to cook 3 more minutes (on same side). Turn chicken, again cover and cook 5 minutes. Remove cover and allow to brown about 4 minutes longer.
This is drained on brown paper and seasoned to taste with salt and pepper.

Fried Chicken
(Country Style)

Gravy
To make gravy pour off excess grease, saving the pan drippings (about 4 tablespoons). Stir in 2 tablespoons flour and brown. Then add 2 cups hot water. Again season to taste. Stir and cook until thick.
Serve with fresh corn, hot biscuits and sliced cold tomatoes.

* The secret is plunging the chicken into the pan of hot water before flouring it.

1 6 lb beef tenderloin
  roasted rare
Make forcemeat using
  1/4 cup each of onion
  butter
  mushrooms
  cognac
  cooked veal
  pork cooked
  cream
  chicken liver
  Mix well

Season with 1/2 tsp. each of
  parsley
  basil
  thyme
  rosemary
  allspice
  pepper

Beef Wellington
Australia

Blend with 1 whole egg and mix thoroughly. Pat on cooked tenderloin. Cover with a rich pastry and bake in hot oven 425 degrees until brown. Slice and serve.

1/4 cup boiling water
1 stick butter

1 1/2 cups pastry flour
1/4 teaspoon salt

Butter Hot Water Pastry
Southern

Melt butter in hot water. Gradually stir in flour. Add salt. Mix quickly, chill and roll out thin and shape over beef wellington. Brush top with butter before baking.

---

1 quart oysters
3 eggs
1 teaspoon onion, grated
1 cup stale bread crumbs

4 tablespoons butter
1 cup buttered bread crumbs
Salt, cayenne pepper to taste
Pinch of allspice and nutmeg

Minced Oysters
Southern

Cook oysters for 6 minutes in their own liquid. Chop up. Add rest of ingredients, saving buttered crumbs for top of casserole. Blend well. Place in baking dish. Top with crumbs. Bake until firm, but moist in a 350° oven.

---

1 fryer (3½ pounds)
Flour, salt, pepper and lard
2 onions, chopped
2 green peppers, chopped
1 small garlic bean, chopped
1½ teaspoons salt
½ teaspoon white pepper
3 teaspoons curry powder

2 No. 2 cans tomatoes
½ teaspoon chopped parsley
½ teaspoon powdered thyme
¼ pound almonds, scalded,
  skinned and roasted
3 tablespoons raisins
2 cups cooked rice

Country Captain
Southern

Cut up chicken in pieces. Remove skin, roll in flour, salt and pepper. Brown in lard. Remove chicken from pan but keep it hot. Saute onion, pepper, garlic and cook slowly. Season with salt pepper and curry powder. Add tomatoes, parsley and thyme. Put chicken in roaster. Pour sauce over chicken, covering completely. (You may have to add some water.) Cover tightly with lid and bake for 45 minutes until chicken is tender. Drop raisins in sauce, sprinkle with almonds. Serve on rice.

Fish Balls
Hawaii

2 pounds boneless cod (ground raw)
1 teaspoon soft butter
¼ teaspoon nutmeg
1½ teaspoon salt
1 beaten egg
¼ cup top milk
1 small onion, minced
½ teaspoon pepper

Mix all ingredients well. Shape into balls. Roll in beaten egg and cracker crumbs. Let chill for 30 minutes in refrigerator. Fry in hot fat slowly until done and brown.

Ham Loaf
Southern

2 pounds lean ham, ground
1 pound lean pork, ground
1 cup cracker crumbs
1½ cups milk
3 eggs
Cloves
Brown sugar

Blend ham, pork and cracker crumbs. Add milk and eggs. Shape like a ham in a baking dish. Dot with cloves. Sprinkle with brown sugar. Bake for 1 hour and 20 minutes in a 350° oven or until done. Serve with horseradish sauce.

Meat Loaf
Southern

2 medium onions (minced)
2 cloves garlic
2 stalks celery with leaves
1 egg
1 pound ground beef
¼ pound sausage
¼ cup milk
½ cup catsup
2 teaspoons salt
½ teaspoon pepper
1½ cups bread crumbs
8 ounces tomato sauce

Thoroughly mix all ingredients except tomato sauce. Shape into meat loaf or put in greased loaf pan. Pour tomato sauce over loaf and bake for 1 hour at 350°.

Avocado Chicken Delight
Bahamas

4 medium sized ripe avocados
2 tablespoons lime juice
4 tablespoons butter
4 tablespoons flour
1 teaspoon salt
2 cups top milk
2 cups chicken cooked and cubed
4 tablespoons pimiento
4 tablespoons chopped green pepper
4 tablespoons cracker crumbs

Cut avocados in half. Remove seed. Sprinkle with lime juice. Melt butter in saucepan. Stir in flour. Add salt and milk. Cook until thick. Add chicken, pimiento, and green pepper. Fill avocados with mixture. Sprinkle with cracker crumbs. Bake for 5 minutes in a 350° oven.

Chicken
Hungarian Style

1 chicken cut up for frying
½ cup butter
Salt and pepper
3 medium onions diced
1 teaspoon paprika
½ cup water
1 cup cream

Season chicken and brown on both sides. Remove from skillet and add onions to skillet. Fry slowly until tender. Return browned chicken, skin side up and sprinkle with paprika. Add water and cover. Cook slowly for 30 to 40 minutes or until tender. Remove chicken pieces to platter. Add cream to skillet mixture. Stir and heat thoroughly. Serve with cooked noodles.

Mounds of fluffy rice.
Serve with this exquisite sauce:

4 tablespoons butter	1½ ounces Calvados or Cognac
¼ cup chopped onion	2 cups consomme
1 whole firm banana, chopped	1 tablespoon cornstarch
2 tablespoons chopped pimento	1 teaspoon curry powder
2 slices diced pineapple	½ cup coconut milk
4 teaspoons chopped shallots	1 teaspoon tomato paste

Pilaf
Middle East

Make sauce by first sauteing onion in butter over low heat. Add other ingredients in order given, mixing the cornstarch in the coconut milk before adding. Simmer over very low heat for 1 hour. Pour over mounds of rice and serve.

In the Middle East slivers of beef, chicken or lamb may be added to the rice.

Thick white sauce made with 2 cups cream, 2 tablespoons butter, 4 heaping tablespoons flour. While hot:

Add:

1 teaspoon salt	1 teaspoon parsley
½ teaspoon celery salt	Pinch nutmeg
White pepper to taste	1 teaspoon lemon juice
2 cups chopped chicken	1 egg
Pinch cayenne pepper	

Chicken Croquettes
Southern

Set aside to cool until very stiff. Shape into croquettes. Dip in beaten egg. Roll in cracker crumbs and fry until golden brown and very hot.

---

5 pounds veal roast	2 tablespoons chopped onions
Salt and pepper	2 cups boiling water
2 tablespoons fat	

6 ounces cooked noodles mixed with
   ½ cup heavy cream

Braised Veal with Noodles
Germany

Sprinkle veal with salt and pepper. Heat fat in heavy roaster. Add onions and brown lightly. Push onions to one side. Add veal and brown on all sides. Add boiling water, cover and simmer 3 hours. Add water, if necessary, to make 1 cup stock when meat is done.

Sauce (Nuremberg Style)

1½ teaspoons powdered mustard	1 cup veal stock
1 tablespoon sugar	2 tablespoons chili sauce
½ teaspoon salt	¼ cup prepared horseradish
1 tablespoon vinegar	2 teaspoons cornstarch (dissolved in water)

Heat all ingredients. Thicken with cornstarch.

---

6 boned chicken breasts, flattened	2 tablespoons flour
1 stick butter, cut in 6 pieces (chilled)	Garlic salt
Flour	Bread crumbs
Beaten egg	

Chicken Kiev
Russia

Place butter, which has been rolled in flour, in center of each breast fillet. Fold over well and skewer. Dredge breast in flour, then beaten egg and roll in bread crumbs. Fry in half butter and half oil until brown. Place in oven, 375 degrees, for a few minutes.

---

1 - 18-pound ham (baked in 350 degree oven for 4 hours. I use fully
   cooked tenderized hams. The additional baking makes them
   delightful.)

Baked Sugar Cured Ham
Southern

SAUCES

Time is that great straightener of crooked ways,
That great curer of angry and unpoised minds,
That great evener of all inequalities.

INDIAN PRAYER

GREAT SPIRIT —

GRANT THAT I
MAY NOT CRITICIZE MY
NEIGHBOR UNTIL I HAVE
WALKED A MILE IN HIS
MOCCASINS

¼ cup brown sugar (firmly packed)
1½ tablespoons cornstarch
⅛ teaspoon salt
1 cup apple cider

¼ cup raisins
8 whole cloves
Dash of cinnamon
1 tablespoon butter

Raisin-Cider Sauce
Southern

Mix sugar and cornstarch in a saucepan. Add remaining ingredients. Cook for 10 minutes, stirring constantly until raisins are plump. Serve hot over baked ham slices.

---

2 cups cream sauce
½ cup tomato sauce
2 egg yolks
¾ cup sugar

¾ cup vinegar
3 tablespoons prepared mustard
½ teaspoon salt

Creamy Mustard Sauce
United States

Combine cream sauce with tomato sauce. Mix egg yolks, sugar and vinegar (blend smooth). Add to white sauce. Stir in mustard and salt. This is good cold.

---

1 cup hot water
½ stick butter
½ teaspoon onion powder
Salt and pepper to taste

1 tlbs. chopped chives or parsley
1 tablespoon cornstarch
2 tablespoons cold water
Yellow food coloring

Butter Sauce for Vegetables
Southern

Cream may be substituted for water, if desired. Bring first 5 ingredients to a boil. Stir in blended cornstarch and water. Cook until thick. Add dash of food coloring and pour over hot vegetables.

---

4 ounces butter
3 tablespoons flour
1 quart chicken stock

3 egg yolks
½ cup thick cream
Salt and cayenne pepper

Sauce Allemande
French

Melt butter. Stir in flour and blend. Add chicken stock and simmer 20 minutes. Mix egg yolks with cream and blend into sauce. Season with salt and pepper.

---

1 pint Allemande sauce

1 cup sherry

Sauce Newburg
French

Use above recipe and add 1 cup sherry.

---

2 ounces butter
1 tablespoon flour
1 pint meat stock (bouillon)
1 tablespoon vinegar

2 tablespoons French mustard
1 tablespoon Maggi
Salt and pepper to taste

Sauce Robert
French

Stir flour into melted butter. Add rest of ingredients and cook, stirring until thick. Garnish with parsley.

---

2 ounces butter
2 ounces flour

1 pint hot milk
Seasoning to taste

Bechamel Sauce
French

Melt butter and stir in flour. Do NOT brown. Stir and blend in hot milk. Use wire whisk. Season to taste.

---

1 pint meat stock
¼ cup sugar
¼ cup vinegar

4 tablespoons mint
Black pepper and salt

Mint Sauce
Southern

Combine all ingredients and thicken with cornstarch.

Remoulade Sauce for Shrimp
French

4 tablespoons lemon juice
4 tablespoons vinegar
4 tablespoons mustard
4 teaspoons horseradish
2 teaspoons salt
½ teaspoon pepper

2 teaspoons paprika
Dash cayenne
2 tablespoons catsup
1 cup oil
½ cup chopped celery
½ cup chopped green onions

Blend ingredients well. Pour over shrimp and let marinate for at least 4 hours.

Italian Meat Sauce
Italian

1 bell pepper
1 onion
½ cup chopped celery
¼ teaspoon marjoram
¼ teaspoon thyme

¼ teaspoon oregano
¼ teaspoon sweet basil
2 bay leaves
2 cups tomatoes or puree

Saute in oil the pepper, onion and celery. Add remaining ingredients and simmer for 15 minutes then add 1 pound ground beef (which has been thinned with water.) Simmer until done. Pour over ravioli or spaghetti.

Sour Cream Watercress Sauce
Southern

½ cup salad dressing
½ cup sour cream
½ teaspoon salt

¼ teaspoon pepper
Few drops of tabasco
½ cup chopped cress

Blend ingredients and serve over fish balls.

Horseradish Sauce
International

1 cup cream, whipped
3 tablespoons horseradish

Dash of cayenne pepper
½ teaspoon sugar

Whip cream, add horseradish, cayenne and sugar. Serve as a side dish to ham loaf or roast beef.

Creole Tomato Sauce
Southern

3 ounces butter
1 medium-sized onion, chopped
3 sliced & chopped bell peppers
4 cups canned tomatoes

1 can sliced mushrooms
2 tablespoons chopped pimento
1 clove minced garlic
Salt and pepper to taste

Saute onion and peppers in butter over low heat for 10 minutes. Add rest of ingredients and simmer for 1 hour over low heat. Thicken if desired.

Original Tartar Sauce
Southern

⅓ cup flour cooked in
1 cup water until thick
2 egg yolks
1 cup salad oil
1 teaspoon salt

2 tablespoons vinegar
2 tablespoons lemon juice
1 teaspoon mustard
1 cup pickle relish

Beat egg yolks into cooked paste of water and flour. Add the salad oil gradually, beating constantly. Then add remaining ingredients and blend well. Chill and serve over fish.

½ cup catsup
2 tablespoons lemon juice
4 teaspoons horseradish
1 teaspoon Worcestershire
sauce

½ cup finely chopped celery
Salt to taste
Dash of onion salt

Mix all ingredients well, and chill.

Shrimp Cocktail Sauce
Southern

---

2 lemons (juiced)
1 tablespoon tarragon vinegar
1 tablespoon Worcestershire
sauce

2 tablespoons soy sauce
7 drops tabasco
1 teaspoon salt
½ pound butter

Melt butter then add rest of ingredients. Serve as a dip for your shrimp.

Butter Shrimp Sauce
Southern

---

2 egg yolks
½ teaspoon salt
Dash cayenne pepper

½ cup melted butter
1 tablespoon lemon juice

Beat egg yolks until thick. Add salt and pepper. Now add 3 tablespoons of the butter gradually. Beat constantly. Then add rest of butter alternately with lemon juice, beating thoroughly after each addition. Serve over hot broccoli or brussel sprouts.

Uncooked Hollandaise Sauce
French

---

1 tablespoon butter
1 1/2 tablespoons grated onion
1/2 cup dry white wine

1 1/4 cups sour cream
Salt and pepper

Melt butter and saute the onion until it is soft but not browned, stirring constantly. Add the wine and simmer until liquid evaporates. Stir in the sour cream; stir and heat thoroughly. Add salt and pepper to taste. This is a great sauce over any boiled vegetable.

Sour Cream Sauce
(For Vegetables)
Asia

1/2 lb. bacon, cut up and fried
3 small onions, cut up fine
3 teaspoons parsley

1/2 lb. ground round of beef
1 cup beef broth

Brown onions in bacon drippings; add parsley. Cook beef in grease with onions and parsley. Keep stirring beef so it remains in small pieces. Add 1 cup beef broth and thicken with cornstarch.

Sauce Mirepoix
Luxembourg

Cook 1/4 cup each chopped onion, carrot and celery in 5 tablespoons butter. When golden, add 1/3 cup flour. Stir over low heat until brown. Add 5 cups hot beef stock, 3 sprigs of parsley, 1/2 bay leaf, 1/2 teaspoon thyme, 1 clove garlic and 1 tablespoon tomato paste. Simmer 1 1/2 hours or until thick enough to coat a spoon. Strain, degrease and season. Add raisins or black olives and serve over meat.

Espagnole Sauce
(Brown)
South America

VEGETABLES
AND
MEAT
ACCOMPANIMENTS

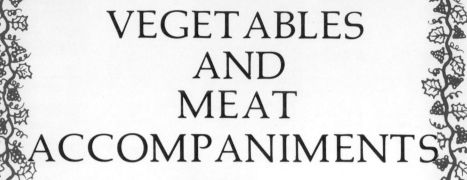

Know the Success Family?

The father of Success is Work;

The mother of Success is Ambi-tion.

The oldest son is Common Sense;

Some of the other boys are Per-severance, Honesty, Thorough-ness, Foresight, Enthusiasm and Co-operation.

The oldest daughter is Character;

Some of her sisters are Cheer-fulness, Loyalty, Courtesy, Care, Economy, Sincerity and Har-mony.

The baby is Opportunity.

Get well acquainted with the "old man" and you will be able to get along pretty well with all the rest of the family.

Use cabbage which has been boiled and seasoned. Make a white sauce and pour over cabbage. (Add other cooked vegetables if desired). Mix well. Place in pastry shells. Sprinkle with cheese and bake until brown, about 20 minutes.

Cabbage Tarts
Austria

SAUCE:
¼ cup butter
1 teaspoon prepared mustard
1 teaspoon Worcestershire sauce
1 tablespoon chili sauce
¼ teaspoon salt and pepper

Mix and heat until melted. Pour over Brussel sprouts.

Deviled Brussel Sprouts
Southern

---

1 large egg plant
3 teaspoons finely chopped green pepper
½ cup finely chopped celery
1 egg
2 cups cracker crumbs
1 small can oysters
1 tablespoon butter
Dash paprika

Boil egg plant until tender (in shell or skin) approximately for 30 minutes. Saute pepper, celery in butter until tender. Add egg and cracker crumbs, oysters and egg plant scooped out of halves. Put mixture back in the half shells. Dash with paprika and bake at 350° for 20 minutes or until brown.

Stuffed Egg Plant
Asia

---

3 tablespoons melted butter
4 tablespoons flour
½ teaspoon salt
⅛ teaspoon pepper
1½ cups milk
½ cup liquid from green beans
½ cup grated American cheese
No. 2 can green beans (2½ cups)

Blend butter, flour and seasoning. Add liquids gradually, stirring constantly. Bring to a boil and cook for 3 minutes. Remove from heat and stir in cheese. Place beans in casserole and pour sauce over. Bake in a 325° oven for 30 minutes.

Green Beans Au Gratin
Southern

---

4 cups boiled mashed rutabaga   Salt and pepper to taste

Place in a cassarole dish. Sprinkle with cracker crumbs and butter. Brown in oven.

Rutabaga
Southern

---

1 cup ground bell pepper
1 cup cracker crumbs
1 cup zippy Cheddar cheese
1 cup milk
Butter

In a casserole place the mixture of bell pepper, cracker crumbs and zippy Cheddar cheese. Pour over this mixture the milk and dot with butter. Place in a 400° oven and bake for 35 minutes.

Bell Pepper Casserole
Southern

French Fried Onions, Deluxe
French

5 large Bermuda onions
Milk
⅔ cup flour
¼ teaspoon salt

2 tablespoons salad oil
⅔ cup water
1 egg white, beaten stiff
Fat for frying

Slice onions in ½ inch rounds. Separate each ring, using the largest ones. Soak for 1 hour in sweet milk. Mix flour, salt, oil and water until smooth. Fold in stiffly beaten egg white. Dry onion slices. Dip in batter and fry until a golden brown and the onion is tender.

Candied Sweet Potatoes
Southern

8 sweet potatoes, thinly sliced
2 cups sugar
2 cups water
½ stick butter

1 teaspoon grated orange rind
Juice of ½ lemon
¼ teaspoon ginger

Bring sugar and water to a boil. Add potatoes and rest of ingredients. Cook until potatoes are done and candied.

Egg Plant Casserole
Southern

1 egg plant, peeled, cubed and
  boiled until tender
2 eggs
Salt and pepper to taste

Cream to moisten well
1 tablespoon onion juice
Cracker crumbs
Butter

Mix egg plant with eggs. Add salt and pepper, cream and onion juice. Thicken mixture slightly with cracker crumbs. Put rest of crumbs on top of casserole. Top with butter and bake for 25 minutes in a 250° oven or until brown.

Surprise Carrot Loaf
Southern

1 cup ground carrots
1 cup ground peanuts
1 cup bread crumbs

1 cup tomatoes
1 tablespoon butter
4 eggs

Grind carrots, peanuts and bread through food chopper. Add tomatoes and butter. Mix well. Beat eggs until foamy. Then add to vegetable mixture. Bake in a greased bread pan in moderate oven 350° for 1 hour.

Curried Fruits
Southern

6 peach halves
6 pear halves
6 pineapple slices
6 sliced apples

1 teaspoon curry powder
1 cup sugar
1 cup juice from fruit
1 stick butter

Place in casserole and bake after sprinkling with sugar and curry for 30 minutes at 350 degrees.

Cauliflower with Tomato Sauce
Southern

1 head cauliflower
1 clove garlic
3 tablespoons cooking oil
Boiling water to cover

½ teaspoon salt
½ cup canned tomatoes
Chopped parsley
Grated cheese

Boil cauliflower in salted water and cook tender. Saute garlic in oil then saute cauliflower (drained) in oil with garlic until brown. Add salt and tomatoes. Simmer for 2 minutes. Sprinkle with parsley and cheese. Serve hot.

1 pound fresh or frozen English
  peas
6 green onions
½ teaspoon salt
Dash of pepper
1 tablespoon sugar

2 tablespoons butter
1 teaspoon flour
¾ cup boiling water
1 tablespoon mixed parsley, tarragon, chives and chervil

Peas and Onions
Southern

Chop onions and add to peas. Cook in hot water until tender. Add seasonings and thicken with flour.

---

3 pounds white cabbage
2 large onions
1½ pounds pork sausage
1 No. 2½ can tomatoes

Black pepper to taste
Grated American cheese
Cracker crumbs

Cabbage Au Gratin
Southern

Dice cabbage and cook in salted water until tender. Crumble sausage in skillet, add onions diced and cook slowly until both are done. Add tomatoes to sausage mixture, add dash of black pepper. Place cabbage in large casserole, pour sausage mixture over cabbage, top with grated cheese and cracker crumbs. Brown for 20 minutes in 400° oven.

---

2 cups cooked spinach
2 well beaten eggs
¾ cup grated cheese
2 tablespoons bacon drippings
1 cup cracker crumbs
1 tablespoon vinegar
4 slices of diced bacon

2 tablespoons chopped onion
2 tablespoons flour
1 cup strained tomatoes
2 tablespoons chopped green
  pepper
Salt and pepper to taste

Spinach Loaf
Southern

Blend first six ingredients well. Pour in baking dish and bake for 25 to 30 minutes at 350°. Make creole sauce out of bacon, onion, flour, strained tomatoes and peppers. Serve with spinach.

---

6 beets, cooked
6 potatoes, cooked
1 onion, minced
3 slices salt pork

½ pound ground beef
⅓ cup meat stock
6 fresh eggs, poached

Red Flannel Hash
Southern

Chop up vegetables fine. Mix all ingredients except eggs. Add meat stock. Cook slowly for approximately 30 minutes. Serve hash with poached eggs on top.

---

2 pounds sauerkraut
4 tablespoons bacon fat
3 apples, quartered
1 sliced onion

Salt to taste
1 teaspoon sugar
2 small grated potatoes
Caraway seed (optional)

Sauerkraut with Apples
German

Add all ingredients and cook in saucepan until onion and apples and potatoes are tender.

Slice potatoes fine. Brown in skillet with fat and season to taste with salt and pepper. Add 1 bell pepper, 1 pimiento and 1 grated onion. Continue to fry slowly until vegetables are tender.

Cottage Fried Potatoes
Southern

Yellow Rice
Spain

4 tablespoons butter (melted)
1 cup long grain rice
3 cups boiling water
1 stick cinnamon
1/2 teaspoon turmeric, ground

pinch of saffron
1 teaspoon salt
1 cup seedless raisins
sugar

Combine melted butter in heavy sauce pan with rice. Stir until coated with butter. Add boiling water and rest of ingredients. Simmer covered for 20-30 minutes until all water is absorbed. Turn out on serving platter. Sprinkle with sugar and serve.

Potatoes Hashed in Cream
Hungarian

4 large cooked potatoes
1 cup cream
Salt and pepper

Cayenne pepper
2 tablespoons butter

Slice potatoes. Add seasoning. Put in baking dish. Dot with butter and bake in a 350° oven for 1 hour.

Potato Crispy Patties
Southern

2 cups cold mashed potatoes
Corn meal

Melted fat

Roll mashed potatoes in corn meal. Shape into patties and fry in melted fat until golden brown and crisp.

Green Corn Fritters
Southern

6 ears of corn
2 eggs
2 tablespoons milk

1 large tablespoon flour
1/4 teaspoon baking powder
Pinch salt

Cut tips of corn off cob. Scrape cob to get milk out of corn. Add rest of ingredients and fry in little cakes the size of a quarter. Be sure and give corn time to get done.

Sauteed Cucumbers and Tomatoes
Southern

Pare 4 large cucumbers
2 tomatoes
Salt and pepper to taste

2 eggs, beaten
Fine cracker crumbs

Cut cucumbers and tomatoes in 1/4 inch slices. Salt and pepper. Dip in beaten eggs and then into cracker crumbs. Heat skillet. Add 1/2 stick butter and saute cucumbers and tomatoes.

Fried Pineapple
Southern

Drain 1 can sliced pineapple. Roll in cracker meal. Fry until a golden brown in bacon fat. Serve hot.

Stuffed Acorn Squash
Germany

Halve the squash and remove the seed and pulp. Cover the bottom of a baking dish with boiling water. Bake squash, cut side down, in a hot oven, 400°, for about 30 minutes or until tender. Sprinkle squash with salt and pepper. Stuff the hollowed centers with mashed potatoes, sausage or dressing. Return to oven and brown.

1 cup white sauce
1 cup cheese, grated
½ teaspoon Worcestershire sauce
1 cup Pureed spinach
3 eggs, separated

Spinach Souffle
Southern

Add cheese and Worcestershire sauce to white sauce. Stir until cheese melts. Stir in spinach and mix thoroughly. Beat egg whites until stiff and the yolks until lemon colored. Add yolks to spinach mixture and fold in whites. Turn into well greased casserole and bake at 400° for 30 minutes.

---

8 apples (winesap)
½ cup raisins
3 tablespoons crushed cornflakes
⅓ cup sugar
½ teaspoon cinnamon
3 tablespoons butter, melted
¾ cup water
¼ cup lemon juice

Breakfast Baked Apples
International

Core apples. Arrange in baking dish which has been well greased. Fill centers with raisins. Combine cornflakes, sugar, cinnamon and butter. Mix until crumbly. Sprinkle over apples. Sprinkle with additional cornflakes. Pour water and lemon juice around apples. Bake in moderately hot oven at 375° for 1 hour, basting every 15 minutes.

---

1 pound ground beef
½ pound ground pork
½ cup grated onion
1 head cabbage
1½ teaspoons salt
½ teaspoon pepper
½ cup raw rice
3 cups water (approx.)

Stuffed Cabbage
Germany

Combine meat and seasonings and rice. Add onion. Wilt cabbage leaves by putting in scalded water. Roll meat mixture up in cabbage leaves. Bake for 1½ hours at 350°. Serve with tomato sauce.

---

5 potatoes
1 tablespoon butter
1 tablespoon flour
1 cup buttermilk
½ teaspoon salt
Pepper to taste

Buttermilk Potatoes
Southern

Dice potatoes and cook until tender, but not mushy. Melt butter in saucepan, stir in flour and seasonings. Add buttermilk and heat only until thickened. Pour over potatoes and toss lightly. Serve while hot.

---

6 medium carrots
½ cup water
1 cup brown sugar
2 tablespoons butter

Candied Carrots
Southern

Boil carrots. Scrape and cut in strips as you would potatoes for frying. Mix other ingredients in baking dish. Place carrots in syrup, covering entirely. Bake until candied.

---

8 winesap apples
3 cups water
1½ cups sugar
¾ cup cinnamon red hot candies

Cinnamon Apples
Southern

Peel apples. Heat water, sugar and cinnamon drops to boiling. Add apples and boil until done, turning once.

Tomato Pudding
Southern

20 oz tomato puree
1 1/2 cups brown sugar
2 cups fresh white bread,
   trimmed and cut in squares
1/2 cup water
1/2 teaspoon salt
3/4 cup butter, melted

Bring sugar, salt, water, and puree to a boil. Place bread in baking dish. Pour melted butter over bread; add hot tomato sauce. Bake in 375⁰ oven for 45 minutes.

Cheese Grits Casserole
Southern

4 cups boiling water
1 cup cheese, grated
   (garlic cheese is great)
2 eggs
1 stick melted butter
1 teaspoon salt
   (garlic salt, if desired)
1 cup grits
1/2 cup milk

Bring water and salt to a boil. Stir in grits and cook slowly for 15-20 minutes, stirring frequently. Then add cheese, blending thoroughly. Beat eggs with milk and stir in butter. Add to grits and cheese. Place in casserole and bake 35 minutes at 350 degrees.

Squash (Stuffed Yellow)
Southern

8 yellow crookneck squash,
   young and tender
1 onion, minced
1 teaspoon sugar
Pinch of salt
6 tablespoons melted butter
10 saltine crackers
5 tablespoons bacon drippings
1/8 teaspoon black pepper

Leave squash whole. Boil the squash for 20 minutes. Let cool. Slice the tops off and scoop out pulp. Mash pulp and mix with other ingredients. Fill squash with stuffing and bake for 15 minutes in 350 degree oven.

Corn (Fried Southern Style)
Southern

8 ears tender corn
1/2 cup water
Salt and pepper to taste
2 tablespoons water
1/4 cup bacon drippings
1/2 cup cream
Cornstarch to thicken

Cut corn off cob and scrape to get juice. Heat skillet with bacon drippings. Add corn, milk, water, salt and pepper. Cook over low heat about 20 minutes. Thicken with cornstarch dissolved in a little water.

Boiled Corn on the Cob
Southern

Shuck 8 tender, young ears of corn. Boil in lightly salted water for 10 minutes. Roll while hot in melted butter. Serve immediately with plenty of butter and pepper, if desired.

Corn Pudding
Southern

6 tablespoons flour
3 tablespoons sugar
1 teaspoon salt
1 1/2 cups milk
2 cups corn, cut and scrape
from the ear
4 tablespoons melted butter
4 eggs

Mix flour and corn. Add sugar, salt and melted butter. Beat milk and eggs together. Stir into corn and pour into a butter pan or baking dish. Bake at 350 degrees for 1 hour, stirring three times during baking to keep the corn from settling to bottom.

1 1/2 cups brown lentils
1 onion finely chopped
1 clove garlic chopped
6 tablespoons butter
salt and black pepper
1 teaspoon ground cumin

Lentils in Butter
Saudi-Arabia

Clean lentils and soak overnight in cold water. In a large sauce-pan fry the onion and garlic in butter until soft. Add the lentils and stir with the butter for several minutes. Add 2 1/2 cups hot water. Season to taste with salt, pepper and cumin. Cover and simmer gently until done. Approximately 1 hour. Serve with a squeeze of lemon if desired.

---

1 cup rice (cooked)
2 cups ground beef
1 large onion, chopped
2 bell peppers, chopped
½ teaspoon celery salt
½ teaspoon sage
1 teaspoon chili powder
½ teaspoon garlic salt
1 can tomato paste
½ pound cheese, grated

Uncle Ben's Rice
Southern

Cook meat, onion and pepper until done. Add rice and seasonings, then tomato paste. Put into casserole dish and top with cheese. Run under broiler until cheese is puffed and melted. Approximately 20 minutes in a 350° oven.

---

1 pound cranberries
3 oranges (whole—seeds removed)
3 apples (whole—seeds removed)
3 cups sugar

Uncooked Cranberry Relish
Southern

Grind cranberries, oranges, apples. Add sugar. Let stand overnight.

---

2 lbs. underripe papaya
1 stick butter
1/4 teaspoon nutmeg
Dash salt
1/4 cup water

Baked Papaya
South America

Peel, seed and quarter the papaya. Place in baking dish, slice butter over them, add nutmeg, salt and water. Cover and bake 45 minutes in 300 degree oven. Delicious!

---

1 medium eggplant
4 cups (8 lbs) chopped tomatoes
1 1/2 cups chopped onion
1 1/2 cups chopped green pepper
1-3 cups raisins
1 cup sugar
1 cup vinegar
3/4 cup water
1 teaspoon tabasco

Egg Plant Chutney
India

Do not peel eggplant; chop into cubes (about 4 cups chopped). Place all ingredients in medium size pot. Bring to boil, stirring occasionally, do not boil. Simmer 10 minutes. Seal in hot sterilized jars. Makes about 3 pints.

2 pounds carrots, pared, cut into
  1/4-inch slices
1 pound turnips, pared, cut into
  1/4-inch slices
2 cups olive oil
1 cup distilled white vinegar

1/2 cup minced pitted green olives
1/2 cup minced pimento
1 clove garlic, minced
  Freshly grown pepper
2 small onions, thinly sliced

Pickled Roots
Cameroon

Cook turnips in boiling salted water to cover in medium-size saucepan until tender, about 8 minutes. Drain; reserve. Cook carrots the same way. Heat oil, vinegar, olives, pimento, garlic and pepper in medium-size saucepan to boiling; reduce heat. Simmer uncovered 5 minutes. Combine reserved carrots, reserved turnips and the onions in large bowl; pour dressing over vegetables. Cool to room temperature. Refrigerate covered 4 hours or overnight.

2 onions, minced
2/3 cup milk
4 large potatoes, boiled
2 parsnips, boiled

Salt and pepper
1 cup cooked, shredded cabbage
1 tablespoon butter
1 tablespoon minced parsley

Colcannon
Ireland

Cook the onion in milk until soft. Mash the boiled potatoes and parsnips together. Season with salt and pepper. Slowly add onions and milk, beating well. Combine with cabbage. Serve garnished with lots of butter and minced parsley.

2 lbs. pumpkin, sliced or in chips
  (should be thin like potato chips)
1 pint vinegar
2 lbs. sugar
1 teaspoon salt

1 teaspoon whole cloves
1 teaspoon whole allspice
1/2 cup crystalized ginger
4 lemon slices
Pieces of stick cinnamon

Pumpkin Chip Pickles
Africa

Place all ingredients in a saucepan, bring slowly to boil and cook until pumpkin is transparent. Lift out the pumpkin and pack in jars with a slice of onion and a little of the ginger. Continue boiling syrup until thick. Spoon over the chips and fill jars with syrup while hot. Seal. Place in refrigerator before serving. For a sweeter chip, instead of vinegar, use 1 cup water and 1 cup lemon juice. Makes 2 1/2 pints.

1 1/2 cups finely chopped, cooked
  spinach
1 tablespoon onion, grated
1 tablespoon grated parmesan
  cheese

1 egg
Dash of allspice
1/2 cup cracker crumbs

Fried Spinach Balls
Africa

Mix ingredients and let stand 15 minutes so crumbs can soak up moisture. Make in balls. Dip in 1 egg beaten with 4 tablespoons water. Roll in cracker crumbs or meal and fry 3 minutes in oil.

Potato Duchess
French

Peel 5 or 6 medium potatoes. Cook until soft and all moisture is gone. Whip up with electric beater. Add 2 tablespoons butter, salt and white pepper to taste. Add a dash of nutmeg, 2 whole eggs and continue beating until fluffy.

1 lb. prunes, soaked overnight in
   1/4 cup Cointreau or Kirsch
1 large melon
2 ripe peaches or mangoes
1 cup seedless grapes or cherries

4 tablespoons powdered sugar
2 tablespoons lemon juice
1 tablespoon orange flavoring
1 tablespoon vanilla extract

Stuffed Melon
Slice off top to use as a cover
International

Scoop out melon, remove seeds and cut up. Mix with all fruits and flavoring. Place back in melon and place top on. Refrigerate for 3 hours. Serve on a buffet. Flowers may be stuck into melon for decoration. Use a knitting needle to make holes!

---

5 cups grated white cheese (Swiss
   type)
4 1/2 cups milk
4 cups flour
1 teaspoon salt

combine with batter
1 1/3 cup milk (canned)
4 eggs
1/2 cup water
3 cups seasoned bread crumbs

Fried Cheese Squares
Switzerland

Bring milk and salt to a scald. Add the flour and stir with a heavy spoon until blended. While hot add cheese. Stir well. When cool enough to handle knead smooth. Press the dough into an oiled pan and spread out to 1/2 inch thick. Chill. Cut in inch squares, dip in beaten egg milk mixture. Roll in crumbs. Fry in deep fat until golden. Serve with soup.

In a bowl combine 3/4 cup each of creamed cottage cheese and sour cream, 1/4 cup flour, 1 tablespoon each of minced parsley and chives, 1 teaspoon salt, 1/2 teaspoon pepper, and cayenne to taste. Beat in 5 egg yolks, 1 at a time, beating well after each addition. In a bowl beat 5 egg whites until they hold stiff peaks. Fold the egg whites into the cheese mixture gently but thoroughly and pour the mixture into a buttered 1 1/2-quart soufflé dish. Bake the soufflé in a preheated moderate oven (350 degrees F.) for 40 to 45 minutes, or until it is puffed and browned. Serves 4 as a luncheon entrée.

Cottage Cheese Soufflé
France

---

4 peaches
4 nectarines
4 apricots
8 plums

2 dozen bing cherries
1 cup water
1 cup sugar

Poached Fruit
France

Heat water in deep kettle. Add 1 cup sugar. Stir until dissolved. Drop in first 3 washed unpeeled fruits. Let come to boil and cover. Simmer for 6 minutes, dip out apricots. Place in deep bowl. At the end of 8 minutes dip out nectarines, at the end of 12 minutes dip out peaches. Now add plums and cherries to the kettle of boiling syrup. Cook 4 minutes only, do NOT let skins pop open. Remove to bowl. Now add 1 cup more of sugar and a drop or 2 of red food coloring. Boil syrup 5 minutes. Pour over fruits, add 2 teaspoons lemon juice. Cool in refrigerator. To serve give each person some fruit, cherries and plums. Elegant for breakfast or dessert.

Asparagus Shortcake
English

2 cups flour
½ teaspoon salt
4 teaspoons baking powder
3 tablespoons shortening
½ cup milk
1 well-beaten egg
Asparagus

Sift dry ingredients. Cut in shortening until mixture resembles coarse crumbs. Combine milk and eggs and add to first mixture and stir dough just enough to blend. Roll ¾ inch thick on lightly floured board. Cut in 3 inch squares and bake in hot oven 425° for 15 minutes. Split shortcake and arrange hot cooked asparagus on one half and top with other half of cake. Pour cheese sauce over all.

CHEESE SAUCE:
2 tablespoons butter
2 tablespoons flour
¼ teaspoon salt
1 cup milk
¼ pound pimiento cheese, cubed

Melt butter, add flour and blend. Add salt. Gradually add milk. Cook until smooth and thick. Add cheese, and stir until cheese is melted.

Baked Stuffed Idaho Potatoes
Southern

6 baking potatoes (baked and scooped out of shell)
½ cup butter
1 cup sour cream
1 tablespoon minced onion
Celery salt to taste
Salt and pepper to taste
½ cup chopped crisp bacon

While potatoes are hot, whip with butter, cream and seasonings. Add more cream if necessary. Spoon into potato shells. Sprinkle with bacon and serve hot.

Apple Fritters
Hungary

Make batter using
1 3/4 cup flour
1/2 can beer
pinch of salt

Dip slices of tart apples (which have been sprinkled with cinnamon sugar and allowed to stand 30 minutes) in batter. Fry in hot oil until light brown. Sprinkle with powdered sugar and serve hot.

Carrots in Wine Vinegar
Southern

2 lbs. slightly, cooked carrots, peeled, cut in 1/4 inch strips
2 cups finely chopped celery
1 thinly sliced bell pepper
1 large red onion, sliced
Marinade:
1 can condensed tomato soup
1 cup sugar
1/2 cup red wine vinegar
1 teaspoon dry mustard
1 teaspoon Worscestershire Sauce
1/2 cup oil

Combine all ingredients. Pour over vegetables. Let stand 24 hours. Keeps well in refrigerator.

Tabouli
Lebanon

3 bunches parsley, minced fine
3 medium tomatoes, chopped
1 bunch green onions, chopped fine
1 cup peppermint leaves, minced
1/4 cup lemon juice
1/4 cup Mazola or olive oil
Salt and pepper to taste

Wash and soak 1 cup cracked wheat, in 2 cups of water for 30 minutes. Combine all ingredients and mix with cracked wheat. Refrigerate. It's marvelous. Cucumbers and radishes may be added if you like.

SALADS AND SALAD DRESSINGS

ENGLISH BLESSING

May your path
Be strewn with flowers,
Memories, friends
And happy hours.
May blessings come
From heaven above,
To fill your life
With peace and love.

    . . An English Blessing

SMILE into the face of the world and a smile comes back— render good service to others and good service is returned to you—show a spirit of helpfulness and that spirit will surely send back aid to you of a like kind—think good thoughts and the same good thoughts will be of you.

The world is a great mirror which truly reflects the thoughts, acts and ambitions of every individual.

Let no one cloud his vision, poison his mind and dwarf his soul with the false imagination that the world is not giving him a square deal.

The only way to avoid getting a square deal from the world is by not giving the world a square deal yourself.

© 1919 S·D·CO. CHI.

Peel very thinly 1 whole ripe pear per person, leaving stem on. Core out center from bottom and fill cavity with blue cheese or Roquefort (left out at room temperature). Put in refrigerator and chill. Serve on bed of endive or watercress. Serve with Lorenzo Dressing.

Stuffed Pears Lorenzo Dressing
Italy

lorenzo dressing

¼ cup vinegar	¾ cup salad oil
2 teaspoons salt	Dash fresh cracked pepper
½ teaspoon English mustard	Dash of Tabasco
2 teaspoons Worcestshire sauce	1/3 cup chili sauce

Mix first seven ingredients thoroughly. Add chili sauce. Stir well just before serving.

Frozen Tomato Chiffon Salad
Southern

1 package whipped topping (2 cups whipped)	1 package lemon jello
1 can tomato paste	½ cup hot water
1 cup mayonnaise	1 jar Durkee's dressing

Dissolve jello in hot water. Cool. Fold in rest of ingredients. Freeze and serve in squares with cucumber mayonnaise.

Cottage Cheese and Pineapple Salad
Southern

2 packages lemon jello	1 cup cottage cheese
1 package lime jello	½ cup mayonnaise
1½ cups hot water	1 can milk, chilled and whipped
1 can pineapple, crushed (drained)	

Combine jello and water, stirring until dissolved. Let partially set. Fold in rest of ingredients. Pour in pyrex dish and chill until firm. Cut in squares.

Asparagus or Fresh Vegetable Mousse
Southern

1 can green asparagus	4 tablespoons water
or 1 cup cucumbers	1 cup mayonnaise
or 1 cup ground cabbage (red or white)	1 cup cream, whipped
or 1 cup celery	1 teaspoon onion salt
or 1 cup cooked broccoli	Juice of 2 lemons
or 1 cup chopped avocado	2 tablespoons chopped pimento
4 tablespoons gelatin	½ cup chopped, slivered almonds

Dissolve gelatin in water (melt over hot water). Stir into mayonnaise, vegetables, whipped cream and other ingredients. Turn into mold. Allow to stand in refrigerator until set. Unmold and serve.

Frozen Fruit Salad
Southern

1 cup cream, whipped	2 bananas, sliced
1 can cherry pie filling	½ cup pecans, chopped
1 can crushed pineapple	½ cup sliced pears
1 can sweetened condensed milk	½ cup sliced peaches
¼ cup lemon juice	

Mix together Eagle Brand milk and lemon juice. Stir until thick. Fold in rest of ingredients and freeze. Serve in squares, frozen, with a dab of mayonnaise.

packages lemon jello   ¼ cup sugar
½ cups hot water
   Blend jello, sugar and water until dissolved.

Gourmet Pickle Mold
Southern

Add: ¼ cup chopped nuts
   ¼ cup chopped celery   1 cup crushed drained pineapple
   ¼ cup chopped pimento   Dash of salt
   ¼ cup chopped dill pickle
   Turn into mold and congeal.

---

tablespoons gelatin   ¾ cup mayonnaise
cup cold water   ½ cup chili sauce
cup chicken broth   1 tablespoon chopped onion
0 hard cooked eggs, chopped   2 tablespoons sweet pickle relish

Molded Egg Salad
Southern

   Dissolve gelatin in cold water. Heat chicken broth and stir in
gelatin. Stir until dissolved. Fold in rest of ingredients. Mold in
favorite container. Chill until firm. Unmold and surround with
omatoes and carrot curls.

---

cups chopped or torn spinach   ¼ cup grated Parmesan cheese
cups torn leaf lettuce   1 egg (which has been sitting in a cup
cups escarole and endive   of hot water for about
½ cup croutons   4 to 5 minutes)

   Crack egg and toss with salad greens, croutons and cheese. Toss
lightly with garlic dressing.

Caesar Salad Garlic Dressing
California

garlic dressing

teaspoon salt   2 tablespoons corn syrup
teaspoon paprika   ¾ cup oil
teaspoon mustard   2 cloves garlic
Dash of cayenne   Fresh cracked pepper
cup lemon juice
   Mix together and pour over greens.

---

2 celery hearts   12 whole peppercorns
½ cups bouillon
   Simmer until tender. Drain and chill. Serve with French dressing.

Celery Hearts (Paris Style)
France

french dressing   Anchovy paste to taste
liced hard cooked eggs   Chopped pimento
   Garnish with eggs and pimento.

---

envelopes plain gelatin   ¼ teaspoon Tabasco
cup cold water   1 teaspoon Worchestershire sauce
cups milk   1 tablespoon horseradish
teaspoons onion powder   ¼ teaspoon black pepper or
cups grated Cheddar Cheese   ¼ teaspoon white pepper
cups fine curd cottage cheese   1 teaspoon celery salt

Molded Buffet Cheese and Cottage Cheese Salad
Southern

   Dissolve gelatin in cold water. Heat milk and stir into gelatin. Add
est of ingredients. Turn into ring mold and chill.

Quilters Potato Salad
Southern

3 large potatoes, cooked
3 hard cooked eggs
4 tablespoons minced onion
Salt and pepper
1 teaspoon dry mustard
1 teaspoon salt

3 teaspoons sugar
2 eggs, uncooked
3 tablespoons melted butter
½ cup hot vinegar
1 cup cream, whipped

Mix first six ingredients. Put next three ingredients in saucepan and cook until thick. Add to first mixture and add whipped cream.

Apple Cider Salad
Southern

1 tablespoon gelatin
2 tablespoons cold water
2 tablespoons lemon juice
¼ cup sugar

1¾ cup cider
1½ cups diced apples
½ cup diced celery

Dissolve gelatin in cold water. Heat cider, lemon juice and sugar. Stir gelatin into cider mixture. Cool and add apples and celery. Turn into molds. Chill in refrigerator until firm.

Shrimp Salad
Southern

2 pounds shrimp
1 cup celery
4 onions (spring)
6 eggs (hard boiled)

2 carrots
1 cucumber
Juice of ½ lemon

Boil shrimp for three minutes in salted water. Cool and shuck. Mince celery, onions, carrots, cucumber and eggs. Combine this with shrimp and add lemon juice. Toss with sharp boiled dressing and serve cold on lettuce leaf.

Greek Salad
Greece

½ head lettuce
2 stalks celery
1 cucumber
2 tomatoes
1 small onion
1 green pepper

1 avocado
4 slices feta cheese
⅓ cup olive oil
1 teaspoon vinegar
Salt, pepper, oregano, olives

Cut up ingredients and combine. Pour oil, vinegar, and seasonings over all. Mix well.

Chicken and Fruit Salad
Hawaii

3 cups white meat of chicken (cooked)
1 orange
1 apple

15 large grapes
15 almonds
1 banana
1 cup mayonnaise

Cut chicken in small pieces. Remove seeds from orange sections. Cut in half. Cut grapes in half, removing seeds. Split almonds. Slice banana. Add the mayonnaise. Mix all ingredients slowly. Serve chilled on lettuce leaf.

2 egg yolks
1 tablespoon Dijon mustard
1/2 lemon
Salt, pepper
1 tablespoon mayonnaise
1 tablespoon sour cream
1 teaspoon mustard dill sauce

Fresh dill
2 cups Lobster meat
1 teaspoon A-1 sauce
Shredded lettuce
Diced mushrooms, asparagus,
    cucumbers, celery

Lobster Salad
Southern

Mix egg yolks and Dijon mustard, add juice and pulp from lemon, salt and pepper. Add mayonnaise, mix; add sour cream, mix; add mustard dill sauce, mix; add fresh dill to taste and mix; add A-1 sauce, mix. Then, according to taste, add some shredded lettuce and mix; add lobster, mushrooms, celery & etc.

---

3 cups shredded cabbage
1 cup thin white sauce
1 tablespoon grated onion

1 tablespoon vinegar
1 teaspoon paprika
3 tablespoons mayonnaise

Hot Slaw
Southern

Fold these ingredients into white sauce and heat. Do not boil. Pour over shredded cabbage.

---

1 envelope plain gelatin
1/2 cup vinegar
1 lemon (juice)
2 cups chopped or ground celery

3 cups chopped or ground cabbage
1/2 cup sugar
2 red bell peppers (ground)
1 teaspoon salt

Perfection Salad
Southern

Dissolve gelatin in 1/2 cup cold water. Heat vinegar, sugar and salt. Stir in gelatin. Pour over mixed vegetables. Let stand in refrigerator until congealed.

Arrangements of cold meats, vegetables, aspic and salads are as different as the housewives and chefs who put them together.
1. In the center, 2 pounds of sliced roast beef, surrounded by aspic.
2. Boiled parslied potatoes.
3. Pickled tiny beets.
4. Radish roses.
5. Steamed asparagus and carrots with a vinaigrette sauce.
6. Steamed cauliflower marinated in vinaigrette sauce. Garnished with raw turnip daisies with carrot centers. (These are just decorations). If you wish you may add sliced pickles, sliced tomatoes, smoked salmon, green olives, salami slices, hard boiled eggs stuffed with pate. Serves 6.

Kalte Feinsch-Mecker-Platte
Iceland

Vinaigrette Sauce
1 cup apple cider vinegar
1 teaspoon dry mustard
1 teaspoon Worcestershire sauce
1/2 teaspoon salt

1 clove of garlic crushed
1/2 teaspoon black pepper
1/2 teaspoon oregano
1 cup salad oil

In a glass jar with a tight lid, mix vinegar with mustard, Worcestershire sauce, salt, pepper, oregano, and garlic and oil. Shake well.

Peanut Salad
United States

1 cup nuts, peanuts
2 cups chopped celery
1 dozen finely chopped ripe
  olives

Enough mayonnaise to bind in-
  gredients
Lettuce
Grapefruit sections

Mix peanuts, celery, olives with mayonnaise. Serve on crisp lettuce. Garnish with grapefruit sections.

String Beans and Nasturtium Salad
Southern

2 cups cold string beans
2 cups chopped greens (lettuce
  escarolle, etc.)
2 green onions

8 nasturtium flowers, chopped
6 tablespoons olive oil
2 tablespoons vinegar
Salt and pepper to taste

Mix all ingredients together. Toss salad lightly.

Salade Nicoise
French

6 cooked potatoes, cold
6 tomatoes
2 cans tuna
Green olives, and black olives
½ head lettuce

4 hard boiled eggs, sliced
1 can anchovy
¼ cup vinegar
¾ cup peanut oil

Cut potatoes in slices. Slice tomatoes. Toss all ingredients together. Serve in large bowl, stirring from the bottom each time.

Raw Hot Spinach
United States

6 tablespoons olive oil
3 tablespoons wine vinegar
2 cloves garlic, crushed
1 tablespoon prepared mustard
Salt to taste
1/4 teaspoon fresh ground pepper

1 1/2 cups thinly sliced mushrooms
6 slices cooked, crumbled bacon
1/4 cup minced, fresh parsley
2 lbs. fresh spinach leaves
*Fresh shrimp, cooked, or fried fish
  is used as a side dish.

Break up spinach in a bowl. Heat rest of ingredients in a large skillet. Pour hot mixture over spinach and serve quickly!

24 Hour Salad
Southern

2 eggs, beaten
4 tablespoons vinegar
4 tablespoons sugar
2 tablespoons butter
2 cups cherries (drained)

2 cups pineapple (drained)
2 oranges, cut
2 cups cut marshmallows
1 cup cream, whipped

Put eggs in double boiler. Add vinegar and sugar. Cool and stir until smooth. Remove from heat. Add butter and cool. When cold fold in fruit mixture and whipped cream. Pour in pan and let stand for 24 hours.

Apple-Raisin Salad
Southern

6 to 8 apples
½ cup seeded raisins
½ cup mayonnaise
1 tablespoon vinegar

Lettuce
Powdered cinnamon
Powdered nutmeg

Core and dice apples. Stir apples and raisins into mayonnaise with vinegar added. Arrange on individual portions of lettuce. Sprinkle with spices.

2 tablespoons plain gelatin
½ cup cold water
3 cups boiling water
2 tablespoons vinegar
⅔ cup thinly sliced celery
⅔ cup ground beets (raw)

2 tablespoons chopped onion
2 tablespoons sugar
1½ teaspoons pepper
¼ teaspoon paprika
⅔ cup ground cabbage

Rosy Beet Salad
Southern

Dissolve gelatin in cold water. Add hot water and stir until clear. Add rest of ingredients, turn into molds, place in refrigerator until congealed.

---

1 package lime jello
¾ cup hot water
¼ cup lemon juice
1 teaspoon onion juice

½ cup sour cream, whipped
½ cup mayonnaise
1 cup chopped cucumber

Cucumber Salad
Southern

Dissolve jello in hot water. Add lemon juice, onion juice and let cool. Fold in whipped cream, mayonnaise and cucumber. Turn into individual molds. Let stand until firm.

---

1 jar bing or black cherries
1 package cherry jello
2 cups hot pineapple juice

1 package cream cheese
½ cup chopped nuts

Black Cherry Salad
United States

Dissolve jello in 2 cups of hot pineapple juice. Stuff bing cherries with cream cheese and nuts mixed. After jello is cooled arrange in mold with stuffed cherries. Let chill until firm.

---

1 package lemon jello
1 can apricots
1 package cream cheese

Juice of 1 lemon
Juice of 1 orange

Apricot Salad
United States

Dissolve the jello in hot juices from the can of apricots, add the orange juice and lemon juice and water (if necessary) to make two cups. Stuff apricots with cheese and congeal in jello mixture.

---

1 package lemon jello
1¼ cups hot water
1 can tomato sauce

1½ tablespoons vinegar
½ teaspoon salt
Dash of pepper

Tomato Aspic
United States

Dissolve jello in hot water. Add rest of ingredients. Chill in mold. For extra special aspic add onion juice, celery salt, Worcestershire sauce or horseradish to taste.

---

2 packages lemon jello
2 cups hot fruit juice
   (drained from fruits)
1 can crushed pineapple
1 can Queen Anne cherries

½ pound grated American cheese
½ pound marshmallows, cut in pieces
1 pint cream, whipped
1 cup mayonnaise
1 cup chopped pecans

Bride's Salad
United States

Melt jello in hot fruit juice. Cool. Fold in rest of ingredients and mold. Lime jello may be used or raspberry, if a different color is desired.

Stuffing for Lettuce
Southern

1 package cream cheese
2 tablespoons Roquefort cheese
1 tablespoon chopped bell pepper
2 tablespoons chopped tomatoes
1 teaspoon onion juice
Salt to taste

Blend all ingredients. Stuff hollowed out lettuce head Chill and cut in ½ inch slices.

Fruit Salad
Southern

3 apples (fresh)
3 pears (fresh)
4 bananas
1 cup celery
4 slices pineapple
2 cups grapes

Cut up fruit. Toss lightly. Serve with whipped cream seasoned with orange juice and a dash of sugar. Serves 12.

Frosted Melon Salad
Southern

1 large cantaloupe
1 cup white seedless grapes
1 package lemon jello
Cream cheese
Heavy cream

Peel cantaloupe. Cut slice from tip end and remove seeds. Fill center with grapes. Pour jello into center. Place top on cantaloupe. Prop up in refrigerator. When chilled frost over with cream cheese. Moisten with cream if necessary. Slice and serve after jello congeals.

Frozen Raspberry-Pear Salad
Southern

1 package raspberry jello
2 packages cream cheese (small)
1 can pears
½ pint cream, whipped
1 cup pecans

Heat 1¾ cups pear juice (add water to make 1¾ cup if necessary). Dissolve gelatin in hot mixture and cool. Whip gelatin mixture then fold in whipped cream, cream cheese, diced pears and pecans. Pour into mold and chill or freeze.

Tomato Salad
Italian

Skin tomatoes and scoop out centers. Season inside with salt pepper and pinch of dill. Place one canned artichoke in each tomato and chill. Half hour before serving, cover with following dressings:

Curried Mayonnaise:
1 pint mayonnaise
1/2 pint sour cream
1 teaspoon curry powder
Lemon juice
Grated onion
Mix and serve over tomatoes.

Frozen Cheese Salad
United States

1 cup cottage cheese
½ cup mayonnaise
1 teaspoon salt
2 tablespoons lemon juice
2 bananas, mashed
½ cup cream
½ cup chopped nuts
½ cup cherries
½ cup diced fruit

Mix all together and freeze in ice tray. Serve on bed of lettuce.

1 cup zwiebach cubes
1 head lettuce
1 avocado
1 can anchovy fillets
1 can artichoke hearts, chopped

1 cup oil
½ cup vinegar
2 tablespoons blue cheese
1 teaspoon celery seed
1 pod garlic

Wickenburg Salad
Southern

Saute zwieback in oil and chopped garlic pod. Let cool. Toss all ingredients together. Garnish with hard cooked eggs.

---

6 tomatoes
1 tablespoon chopped parsley
6 ounce American cheese

6 eggs
Salt and pepper to taste

Breakfast Salad
Southern

Scoop out tomatoes with spoon. Simmer tomato pulp with chopped parsley until a thick paste. Scramble eggs and cheese together in skillet. Mix with tomato mixture. Salt and pepper to taste. Restuff tomatoes and serve for breakfast.

---

1 can Bartlett pears
½ cup cinnamon drops
1 tablespoon vinegar
1 package plain gelatin

2 tablespoons cold water
Mayonnaise
Nuts

Cinnamon Pear Salad
Southern

Drain juice from pears. Heat with vinegar and cinnamon drops until cinnamon has melted. Dissolve gelatin in cold water. Stir into hot mixture. Pour over pears. Chill until firm. Serve topped with mayonnaise and nuts.

---

1 package macaroni
1 bunch water cress or celery
4 to 6 hard cooked eggs
4 green onions
2 slightly green tomatoes

Salt and pepper to taste
1 bell pepper, chopped
Enough mayonnaise to moisten salad

Macaroni Salad
Southern

Mix all ingredients together. Serve on lettuce leaves.

---

1 lb washed fresh spinach
1 can drained bean sprouts

1 cup sliced water chestnuts

Dressing:
3/4 cup sugar
1 Tbs worcestershire sauce
1/4 cup vinegar
1/4 tsp pepper

3/4 cup salad oil
1/4 cup minced onion
1/4 cup tomato catsup
1/4 tsp salt

Water Chestnut and Spinach Salad
Japan

Mix the dresing ingredients and pour over vegetables. Let stand 30 minutes. Serve garnished with crisp bacon and hard cooked eggs.

1/2 cup oil
1/2 cup white vinegar
1 1/2 cup sugar
heat until sugar dissolves

1 no 2 1/2 can sauerkraut (drained)

2 cups diced celery
1/2 cup diced onion
1/2 cup diced green peppers
1/2 cup diced pimento
1 teaspoon caraway seeds
1 teaspoon celery seed

Sauerkraut Salad
Poland

Heat sugar, vinegar and oil. Chop vegetables add to sauerkraut and mix with rest of ingredients.

Let stand 3 hours. Will keep 2 weeks.

Bean Salad
Southern

2 cups drained wax beans
2 cups drained, washed kidney beans
2 cups drained cut green beans
½ cup chopped celery
¼ cup chopped onion
¼ cup chopped parsley

Salt and pepper to taste
1 teaspoon Worcestershire sauce
¾ cup vinegar
¾ cup sugar
¾ cup oil
3 tablespoons chopped crisp bacon

Marinate beans with combined ingredients except bacon. Serve with crisp bacon as garnish.

Roquefort Cheese Dressing
French

3 tablespoons of oil
1 tablespoon vinegar
1 teaspoon English mustard
1 teaspoon Worcestershire sauce
½ teaspoon cayenne pepper

½ teaspoon salt
Roquefort cheese
Garlic
4 hard boiled eggs
Lettuce

Combine oil, vinegar, mustard, Worcestershire sauce, cayenne pepper and salt. Rub Roquefort cheese in oil mixture until smooth and there are no lumps. Rub bowl with garlic then put 2 or 3 small pieces of garlic in oil mixture. Serve on lettuce wedges with hard boiled eggs.

Dutch Potato Salad Dressing
German

1 teaspoon flour
2 tablespoons brown sugar
½ cup water

¼ cup vinegar
1 cup mayonnaise

Combine ingredients and cook until thick. Pour dressing over potato salad.

Russian Dressing
Russia

1 cup mayonnaise
2 hard cooked eggs, minced
1 tablespoon chopped green pepper

1 tablespoon chopped green onions
⅓ cup chili sauce

Combine all ingredients. Serve on tomato and egg salad or on plain lettuce.

Thousand Island Dressing
United States

1 cup mayonnaise
⅓ cup chili sauce
⅓ cup whipped cream

2 tablespoons chopped sour pickles
1 chopped pimiento

Mix these ingredients well. Serve on seafood, ham, asparagus salad or macaroni.

Tomato French Dressing
Southern

1 cup salad oil
½ cup vinegar
2 teaspoons salt
2 tablespoons Worcestershire sauce
2 tablespoons prepared mustard

1 tablespoon black pepper
½ cup sugar
1 can tomato soup, condensed
1 clove garlic, minced
1 onion, chopped

Mix thoroughly in quart jar. Keeps indefinitely. Delicious over tossed salad or slaw.

⅓ to ½ cup sugar
1 teaspoon grated onion
1 teaspoon paprika
1 teaspoon salt

1 teaspoon dry mustard
1 teaspoon celery seed
¼ cup vinegar
1 cup salad oil

Glazed Sweet Fruit Salad Dressing
Southern

Combine sugar, onion, paprika, salt, mustard, celery seed and 1 tablespoon vinegar. Gradually add oil alternately with remaining vinegar. This makes a thick glossy dressing that is wonderful over fresh fruit.

---

2 teaspoons dry mustard
⅛ teaspoon cayenne pepper
2 tablespoons flour
2 cups boiling water
½ cup cold water

2 teaspoons salt
4 tablespoons sugar
¼ cup lemon juice
4 egg yolks

Eat and Grow Thin Salad Dressing
United States

Mix dry ingredients. Beat eggs and mix with the cold water. Now blend in the dry ingredients. Add the boiling water and stir mixture as you are adding the water. Add lemon juice. Place in heavy saucepan and cook over low heat until smooth. (Do not let boil or it will curdle.) When thick store in refrigerator.

---

4 eggs, well beaten
⅔ cup vinegar
4 teaspoons sugar
½ teaspoon dry mustard

2 teaspoons prepared mustard
Dash cayenne and black pepper
2 tablespoons butter

Boiled Dressing
Southern

Put all ingredients except butter in saucepan. Cook over low heat until mixture thickens—stirring constantly. Lastly stir in butter.

---

1 cup sour cream
½ cup ground parsley
½ cup ground spring onions
½ cup ground celery
½ cup chopped cucumbers
1 teaspoon lemon juice

1 teaspoon garlic salt
1 tube anchovy paste
1 cup mayonnaise
1 teaspoon tarragon
Salt and pepper to taste

Green Goddess Dressing
United States

Mix all ingredients and serve over vegetables.

---

1 teaspoon salt
½ teaspoon paprika
¼ teaspoon mustard
Dash of cayenne

1 teaspoon plain gelatin
¼ cup cold milk
½ cup hot milk
4 tablespoons lemon juice

Slimming Mayonnaise
Southern

Dissolve gelatin in cold milk. Then add the hot milk and stir until dissolved. Add rest of ingredients. Chill until half congealed. Beat until fluffy. (If it needs thinning add a little more milk or lemon juice.)

BREAD AND SUCH

YOU are the sculptor of your own existence.

The goal you set is the model by which you work and the present is the clay with which you are ever working—molding your to-morrow by your deeds of today.

You can't remodel the past —the future is only yours to anticipate—but NOW is your time—and my time— to shape as we will.

1 cup flour
2 cups bran cereal
3 tablespoons baking powder
½ teaspoon salt
2 eggs, beaten

1 cup milk
4 tablespoons melted butter
½ cup brown sugar
¾ cup fig preserves

Fig Bran Muffins
International

Mix all together and bake in muffin tin in a 450° oven for 20 minutes.

---

1 cup sifted flour
1½ teaspoons baking soda
1 teaspoon salt
1 teaspoon baking powder

½ cup brown sugar
2 cups sour milk
2 cups graham flour
4 tablespoons melted fat

Graham Muffins
International

Mix dry ingredients. Add milk to fat. Beat thoroughly. Bake in muffin tins at 400° until done.

---

1 cup flour
1½ cups corn meal
1 teaspoon salt
5 teaspoons baking powder
2 tablespoons sugar

1½ cups cooked oatmeal
1 egg
2 tablespoons shortening
1 cup milk

Oatmeal Bread
Southern

Sift together flour, corn meal, salt, baking powder and sugar. Add oatmeal. Add beaten egg, melted shortening and milk. Mix well and bake in greased shallow pan in medium oven (375°) for 40 to 45 minutes.

---

2 cups flour
4 teaspoons baking powder
½ teaspoon salt
3 tablespoons sugar
½ teaspoon allspice

2 eggs
1 cup milk
3 tablespoons melted butter
½ cup thick apple sauce

Apple Sauce Muffins
Southern

Mix dry ingredients. Beat eggs with milk and melted butter. Stir quickly into dry ingredients. Add apple sauce last. Blend quickly. Do not beat smooth. Bake in a 400° oven for 20 minutes.

½ cup margarine, melted
1 cup banana puree
1 cup sugar
2 cups flour

1 teaspoon soda
½ teaspoon salt
2 eggs
1 cup pecans (chopped)

Banana Nut Bread
Southern

Mix all ingredients well. Pour in two bread pans. Bake in a 450° oven for 15 minutes then turn heat down to 350° and bake approximately 45 minutes more until bread is done.

Beat 2 eggs lightly with 1 cup rich milk. Dip bread (several days old) into mixture. Coat evenly. Lower into deep fat and fry to golden brown. Serve with butter and syrup.

French Toast
French

Basic Biscuit Dough
Southern

2 cups flour
2 teaspoons baking powder
1 teaspoon salt

1 tablespoon sugar
Shortening the size of an egg
Enough milk to moisten

Sift dry ingredients together. Blend in shortening and moisten with milk. Do not over mix. Turn out on floured board, cut out and bake in a 450° oven until brown, about 12 minutes.

Corn Pone
Southern

1 cup hominy, drained
1 tablespoon margarine
3 eggs

1 pint sweet milk
Corn meal

Heat hominy in pan with margarine until melted. Beat eggs into sweet milk and add to hominy. Heat to scalding. Add corn meal until it is thick enough to shape into pones. Grease hands with bacon fat and shape into small pones. Lay on greased pan and bake in a 400° oven until brown and done.

Funnel Cakes
German

2 cups milk
2 eggs
½ teaspoon baking powder

Pinch salt
Enough flour to make a thin
batter (about 2½ cups)

Beat the eggs well. Add milk. Sift salt and baking powder into a little flour. Add to the egg-milk mixture. Continue adding flour until you have a thin batter. Have hot fat ½ to 1 inch deep in pan. Put batter into funnel and then into hot fat, beginning in the center of the pan and turning the stream around in a gradually increasing circle. Being careful not to overlap batter. Fry a golden brown and serve with a tart jelly.

Spoon Bread
Southern

1 cup corn meal
1 teaspoon salt
1½ tablespoons melted butter

4 eggs, separated
1 teaspoon baking powder
3 cups milk

Add corn meal to milk. Stir until smooth. Add salt. Cook until a thick mush. Stir in melted butter and cool. Add beaten egg yolk and baking powder. Fold in stiffly beaten egg whites. Bake in buttered casserole dish for 45 minutes at 375°.

Egg Bread
Southern

2 cups corn meal
1 teaspoon baking powder
½ teaspoon soda
1 teaspoon salt

1 beaten egg
1½ cups buttermilk
1 tablespoon melted butter

Sift together dry ingredients. Combine the milk and egg. Add to dry ingredients then add melted butter. Pour into a well greased pan. Bake in a 425° oven about 25 minutes.

Home-Made Crackers
International

1 cup flour
2 teaspoons butter
½ teaspoon salt

1 egg beaten
¼ cup milk

Combine all ingredients. Roll thin and sprinkle with salt. Cut into squares. Pierce surface of each cracker with fork. Bake in a 350° oven until golden brown and crispy.

2 cups sifted flour
1 teaspoon salt
3 teaspoons baking powder
3 tablespoons shortening

1 cup cold mashed potatoes
1 egg
⅓ cup milk

Potato Scones
Scotland

Sift together to flour, salt and baking powder. Cut in shortening, then mix in the cold potatoes. Beat the egg and add to the milk, and add to potato mixture. Mix only enough to blend well. Roll out to ⅜ inch thickness on floured board. Cut in squares. Bake slowly on hot griddle turning several times. Split and toast before serving.

1 cup raisins
3 cups flour
6 teaspoons baking powder
¾ teaspoon salt
2 tablespoons sugar

2 tablespoons shortening
3 eggs
1 cup milk
½ cup crisp crumbled bacon

Raisin Muffins
Southern

Work shortening into dry ingredients. Combine eggs and milk. Add raisins and bacon and blend well. Bake in a 450° oven for 25 minutes.

1 cup corn meal
1 cup whole wheat flour
1 cup white flour
1 teaspoon salt

2 teaspoons soda
2 cups sour milk
¾ cup molasses
1 cup raisins (if desired)

Boston Brown Bread
United States

Mix and sift dry ingredients. Add molasses and milk. stir until well mixed. Turn into a well buttered mold and steam 3½ hours. Fill mold 2/3 full. Cover (with waxed paper). Place molds on racks. Pour water in to ½ way up around mold. Cover closely and steam.

2 cups flour
1½ teaspoons sugar
½ teaspoon salt

1 cake yeast
¾ cup lukewarm water
1 tablespoon melted shortening

Snow Biscuit
Southern

Sift together the dry ingredients in a bowl. Dissolve yeast in warm water. When dissolved, add to dry ingredients, then add shortening. Knead for five minutes then roll out one-half inch thick on lightly floured board. Cut in rounds and let rise until double in size. Bake in 425° oven until brown.

1 cup hot water
1/3 cup sugar
1 whole egg
3½ cups flour
¼ cup oil

1 teaspoon salt
1 cake yeast - dissolved in 1/3 cup
    warm water
Dash yellow food coloring, if desired

Rolls or Basic Bread Recipe
Southern favorite—

Put all ingredients in mixing bowl - except 1 cup flour and yeast mixture. Beat smooth. Add yeast mixture and coloring. Allow to rise 1 hour or until double in size.

Dump rolls out and knead on lightly floured board (with 1 cup flour you have reserved) until smooth. Roll out ½ inch thick and cut with small cutter. Place on greased baking sheet. Allow to rise until double in size. Bake in 350 degree oven for 15 to 20 minutes or until brown.

We brush rolls with lots of melted butter the last 5 minutes of baking.

6 cups sifted flour
2 medium sized Irish potatoes
1 cup potato water
2 eggs with milk enough to make 1 cup liquid

½ cup melted shortening
¾ cup sugar
2 teaspoons salt
2 yeast cakes
¼ cup lukewarm water

Old Fashioned Light Bread
Southern

Boil potatoes until tender. Mash and add the potato water in a bowl. Add shortening, sugar and salt, and mix well. Dissolve yeast in lukewarm water. When potato mixture is lukewarm add yeast mixture. Blend well. Add the eggs and milk which have been well mixed. Measure flour into large mixing bowl and add the liquid, a little at a time; blending well, making a soft dough. Place dough on lightly floured board and knead for ten minutes. Let rise in a warm place until double in bulk. Knead few minutes again. Make into loaves and let rise until double in size. Bake in a 400° oven for 20 minutes and then reduce heat to 300° and bake 25 minutes longer. Be sure the pans are greased well.

1 cup scalded milk
¼ cup butter
2 tablespoons sugar
½ teaspoon salt

1 cake yeast softened in ¼ cup water
Whites of 2 eggs beaten stiffly
3¾ cups flour

Bread Sticks
Italian

Add butter, sugar and salt to scalded milk and let cool. Add yeast, egg whites and flour. Let rise for 1 hour then knead. Roll dough out to ½ inch thickness and cut in strips and roll into 8 inch long sticks. Let rise until double in size. Bake in 400° oven 8 or 10 minutes then reduce heat to 350° and let dry out. Serve with ravioli or spaghetti.

1¾ cups flour
¾ teaspoon salt
¼ cup sugar
2 teaspoons baking powder

2 eggs
4 tablespoons melted margarine
¾ cup milk or liquid
1 cup flour-coated blueberries

Blueberry Muffins
United States

Sift dry ingredients in bowl. Stir in liquids. Beat smooth. Fold in blueberries. Bake in a 425° oven for 15 minutes.

1 cup boiling water
½ cup milk
3 tablespoons fat
1 cake yeast
1 tablespoon sugar
1½ teaspoon salt
4 cups sifted flour
Cornmeal

English Muffins
English

Add boiling water to milk and fat. Stir and cool to lukewarm. Add yeast crumbled with sugar. Add salt and half the flour. Beat well. Cover and let rise until foamy. Add flour to make soft dough. Knead 2 minutes on floured board. Place in greased bowl and cover. Let rise until double.

Roll to ¾ inch thickness and cut in 3½ inch rounds. Sprinkle with cornmeal. Bake 20 minutes on well greased hot griddle.

1 cup water
¼ cup cornmeal
1 tablespoon shortening
¼ cup molasses

1 teaspoon salt
1 cake yeast
¼ cup warm water
3¾ cups flour

Cornmeal Molasses Rolls
Southern

Bring water to a boil and add cornmeal gradually, stirring constantly. Add shortening, molasses, and salt. Let stand until lukewarm. Add yeast cake to ¼ cup warm water. Combine with the cornmeal mixture. Stir in the flour to make a stiff dough. Knead well. Place in a greased bowl and let rise until double in bulk. Knead well again and make into rolls. Let rise for 1½ hours and bake in a 450° oven until brown.

1 package dry yeast
1/4 cup lukewarm water

1 egg
1/2 cup honey
1 tablespoon ground coreander

1/2 teaspoon ground cinnamon
1/4 teaspoon ground clove
1 1/2 teaspoon salt
1 cup lukewarm milk
6 tablespoons melted butter
4 1/2 cup flour

Honey Bread
Middle East

Dissolve yeast in warm water and set aside.

Beat egg, honey and spice together until fluffy. Add the yeast mixture, warm milk and melted butter. Stir in flour. Knead the dough until smooth. Add a little oil to your hand to keep dough from sticking. (don't add more flour. Let rise until double in size. About 1 hour. Punch down and knead for a couple more minutes. Shape into round loaf or place in a greased loaf pan. Let rise again until double. About 1 1/2 hours. Bake in 300 degree oven 1 hour. Warm. Serve with butter and honey.

2 cups oatmeal (uncooked)
2 cups buttermilk
2 eggs
1 cup sifted flour

1 teaspoon soda
1 teaspoon baking powder
1 teaspoon salt
2 tablespoons melted butter

Oatmeal Griddle Cakes
Scotland

Mix oatmeal and buttermilk. Let stand overnight. Add rest of ingredients, blending only until smooth. Bake on hot greased griddle. Serve with cranberry syrup.

2 eggs
¼ cup sugar
½ cup whipping cream, whipped

2½ cups flour
2 tablespoons melted butter
1 teaspoon baking powder
1 teaspoon cream of tartar

Swedish Donuts
Sweden

Beat eggs until light and fluffy. Add sugar and beat well. Add melted butter, baking powder and cream of tartar, beating well to blend. Add alternately whipped cream and flour. Makes a very stiff dough. Roll out ½ inch thick and cut into donuts. Fry in deep fat. Delicious hot or cold.

1 pint whipping cream
¼ cup vinegar or orange juice
2 cups sifted flour

4 tablespoons melted butter
½ cup ice water

Swedish Waffles
Sweden

Whip cream (not too stiff). Fold in vinegar, flour, melted butter and ice water. Bake in waffle iron.

Crispy Waffles
United States

2 cups flour
1 teaspoon soda
1 tablespoon sugar
1 teaspoon salt
2 eggs, separated

¼ cup vinegar
1¾ cups sweet milk
4 tablespoons melted shortening

Sift dry ingredients. Beat egg yolks, vinegar and milk together. Add dry ingredients and then melted shortening. Blend well. Fold in egg whites, stiffly beaten. Bake on hot waffle iron.

Thistle Down Balls
Southern

1 package yeast
1½ cups water (warm)
4 cups flour

¾ stick butter, melted
½ teaspoon sugar

Dissolve yeast in warm water. Stir in flour, butter and sugar. Knead smooth and let rise. Pinch off small pieces of risen dough and drop into hot fat and fry. Roll in powdered sugar.

Raised Donuts
United States

1 yeast cake (dissolved in water)
1 cup milk (scalded and cooled)
2 beaten eggs

1 teaspoon salt
¾ cups sugar
½ cup shortening
About 5 cups flour

Cream shortening and sugar. Add beaten eggs, salt, milk and yeast. Stir in flour. Knead until smooth. Roll out and let rise 1 hour. Fry in deep fat until nicely browned. Ice with following: blend until smooth 1½ cups confectioners sugar, 2 tablespoons hot milk, ½ teaspoon butter and ½ teaspoon vanilla. Glaze donuts when cold.

Fluffy Hot Cakes
Southern

1 egg
¾ cup and 2 tablespoons milk
2 tablespoons melted shortening

1 cup flour, sifted
½ teaspoon salt
2 tablespoon baking powder
2 tablespoon sugar

Beat all ingredients until smooth. Bake on griddle until fluffy and brown. Turn only once.

Swiss Butter Cream Breakfast Rolls
Switzerland

1 cake yeast dissolved in
1/4 cup lukewarm water
1 stick butter (melted)
1/2 tsp salt
1/2 cup sugar

1 cup thick sour cream (at room temperature)
1 egg yolk
1/2 tsp vanilla
approx. 3 1/2 cups flour

Combine sour cream, butter, egg yolk, and salt, vanilla and sugar. Beat until light. Add yeast dissolved in lukewarm water. Work in flour and beat until dough leaves side of bowl. Refrigerate over night. Knead until smooth adding as little flour as possible. Shape into buns, rolls, bread, or cut in triangles, sprinkle with sugar and roll into croissants. Bake in 400⁰ oven 15 minutes, or if a loaf bake at 350⁰ for 40 minutes. Serve hot with butter and marmalade or raspberry jam.

2 eggs, slightly beaten
2 cups buttermilk
1 cup cornmeal
2 cups flour, whole wheat
2 tablespoons shortening,

melted
1 teaspoon salt
1 teaspoon soda
3 teaspoons baking powder
Little water

Whole Wheat Griddle Cakes
United States

Dissolve soda in a little cold water. Blend dry ingredients; add eggs, buttermilk and shortening. Add soda and stir just enough to blend. Mixture should be lumpy. Fry on hot griddle.

---

1 cake yeast
¼ cup boiled water, cooled
¾ cup flour

2 cups boiled water
1½ teaspoons salt
6 cups flour

French Bread
French

Knead first three ingredients into a ball. Set the ball in a bowl containing the 2 cups of boiled water that has been cooled to lukewarm. When ball floats add the salt and the rest of the flour. Knead for 15 minutes and let rise until double in bulk. Knead again, shape into long loaves. Cut furrow in each loaf and let rise until double in bulk. Bake for 10 minutes at 450° then reducing heat to 300° and bake for 50 minutes. Brush with beaten egg white.

---

4 cups flour
1 teaspoon salt
¼ cup sugar
2 yeast cakes

1 cup milk
1 egg
1½ cups butter

Danish Pastry
France

Sift flour and mix with sugar and salt. Mix yeast with a little milk. Add the rest of the milk and the beaten egg to flour and sugar. Beat until smooth with a wooden spoon. Roll out the dough on a baking board to one finger thickness. Spread small pieces of butter on 2/3 of the dough. (Butter must be at room temperature. If too soft it melts into dough, so be cautious. Fold dough into 3 layers, first the part without butter. Roll out again, using more butter and repeat this three or four times. Let rise the last time you fold it ½ hour. Shape pastry and let rise 20 minutes longer. Brush with egg white and bake in 450° oven until brown. May add jelly, powdered sugar after pastries are baked.

---

1 cup flour
2 tablespoons powdered sugar
½ teaspoon salt

1 cup milk
2 eggs
1 tablespoon melted butter

Crepes Suzette
French

Sift dry ingredients together; add eggs, milk and butter and stir until well blended. Fry until brown on grill. Pancakes should be very thin. Roll up and serve with sauce. Pour brandy over pancakes and burn brandy if desired.

SAUCE: 1 cup sugar, ½ cup butter, juice and grated rind of 2 oranges, 1 tablespoon lemon juice and flavor with sherry wine. Combine all ingredients except sherry and boil until a syrup forms. Add sherry. Pour over pancakes.

Blini
(Russian Pancakes)

1 cup sour cream
1 cup cottage cheese
4 eggs, separated

¾ cup flour
1 tablespoon sugar
¼ teaspoon salt

Mix sour cream and cottage cheese. Stir in flour and well beaten egg yolks. Beat smooth and add salt and sugar. Fold in stiffly beaten egg whites. Fry on well greased griddle.

Butter Pecan Rolls
Danish

DOUGH:
1 egg
2 cakes yeast
2 tablespoons lukewarm water
1 cup hot water
1 teaspoon salt
1½ tablespoons shortening, melted

½ cup sugar
3½ cups flour

PECAN TOPPING:
½ cup brown sugar
½ cup chopped nuts
1 teaspoon cinnamon
½ cup white corn syrup

Beat egg. Add salt, melted shortening and sugar and hot water. Beat until lukewarm. Add yeast softened in lukewarm water and flour. Knead slightly. Let rise until double in bulk. Punch down. Roll out in big rectangular sheet ¼ inch thick. Spread with cooled melted butter. Roll up jelly roll fashion. Cut off in ½ inch lengths. Butter sides of muffin tins. Pad with soft brown sugar combined with the cinnamon. Pour ½ tablespoon syrup into each muffin hole. Over this place a layer of pecans. Now place dough on this. Let rise 1 hour before baking. Bake in 375° oven until brown. Turn out of pans immediately. Serve hot or cold.

Hot Cross Buns
English

1 cake yeast
1 cup lukewarm water
6 cups flour
¾ cups melted shortening
3 beaten eggs

1 cup sugar
1 teaspoon cinnamon
1 teaspoon ginger
1 teaspoon nutmeg
1 teaspoon clove

Mix the yeast, water and 1 cup flour. Let rise until bubbly. Add the rest of the flour and other ingredients, in order. Let rise until double in bulk. Shape into round, flat buns. Brush with egg white. Cut cross on bun with scissors and bake in a 450° oven for 8 minutes.

Popovers
Southern

2 cups flour, sifted
3 eggs

1 tsp salt
2 cups milk

Beat eggs and milk together and gradually add flour. Keep on beating for about 5 - 10 minutes.

Have muffin tins hot and well greased and oven heated to 450⁰. Put batter in hot pans half full. Bake 20 minutes. Turn off oven and let bake 15 minutes longer. Keep warm and serve with lots of butter.

Soft Egg Bread
Southern

Very delicate, much more custard-like than spoon bread. Mix 1 cup corn meal with 1 quart buttermilk. Add 3 beaten eggs (4 are better) and 1/2 teaspoon salt. Bake in a slow oven in a well-buttered pudding or souffle dish until a silver knife thrust into it comes out clean.

2 eggs
1 teaspoon soda
1 tablespoon sugar
1 teaspoon banana extract
1/4 cup melted butter

2 cups buttermilk
1 teaspoon salt
2 teaspoon baking powder
2 cups sifted flour
1 cup thinly sliced bananas

Banana Hot Cakes
Southern

Beat eggs until light and fluffy. Blend in buttermilk, soda, salt, sugar, baking powder and banana extract. Beat until smooth. Gradually blend in flour and mix to smooth batter. Fold in melted butter and banana slices. Cook on lightly oiled griddle and serve immediately with favorite syrup and whipped butter or banana-flavored whipped cream. Makes 10 to 12 cakes.

3/4 cup pecans
1 cup dates
1 1/2 teaspoons soda
1/2 teaspoon salt
1/4 cup shortening melted

3/4 cup boiling water
2 eggs
1/2 teaspoon vanilla
1 cup sugar
1 1/2 cups sifted flour

Date Nut Bread
Southern

Beat eggs and add to dry mixed ingredients.

Grease 4 soup cans with oil. Fill 2/3 full. Cover and bake at 350 degrees for 10-25 minutes.

Bring to a boil:
2 cups water
1/4 cup cider vinegar
1/4 cup molasses

1/2 cup oil
1 square (1 oz.) unsweetened chocolate
Cook mixture to lukewarm.

Black Bread
Russia

Combine 2 envelopes of dry yeast with 1/2 cup lukewarm water and add 1 teaspoon sugar. Let stand 10 minutes.
Combine 4 cups rye flour with 3 cups white flour. Toss with fork until blended. Take 3 cups of the rye flour mixture (reserving rest to use when kneading bread) and add 2 cups whole bran cereal, 2 tablespoons caraway seed, 1 tablespoon salt, 2 teaspoons of instant coffee, 2 teaspoons freeze-dried minced onion, and one teaspoon fennel seed. Stir in the cooled water-vinegar-molasses mixture and add yeast mixture. Beat dough with dough hook or spoon for about 2 minutes. Add enough of the remaining rye and white flour to make a soft dough. Make a ball and grease well. Let rise in a warm place for one hour, then knead the dough with the rest of the flour mixture for about 15 minutes until it is smooth and resilient.
Shape into 2 loaves (round) and fit into well greased 8 inch cake pans. Oil the top of the bread, and let rise for 1 1/2 hours or until doubled. Bake in 350 degrees oven 50 minutes. Serve with butter, sour cream or cheese.
Loaves may be glazed with a cornstarch wash made by bringing to a boil 1/2 cup water and 1 teaspoon cornstarch. Brush on baked bread and return to the oven for 5 minutes.
Wrap bread with saran wrap to retain moisture. This slices beautifully.

DESSERTS AND PARTY FAVORITES

IRISH BLESSING

May the road
rise to meet you.
May the wind be
always at your
back, May the sun shine
warm upon your face,
the rains fall soft upon
your fields and until we
meet again . . . may God
hold you in the palm
of His Hand.
        . . . An Irish Blessing

½ cup sugar
1 cup port wine
Ice cream and black bing cherries

1 cup black bing cherry juice
½ cup cherry brandy

Cherries Jubilee
United States

Heat first 3 ingredients. Add brandy and ignite as you spoon over ice cream and cherries.

Layer of sponge cake
Layer of strawberry jam
Layer of sponge cake soaked with sherry
Layer of custard (rum flavored)
Sprinkle with candied cherries and orange peel

Layer of sponge cake
Spread with sweetened whipped cream flavored with rum or brandy
Sprinkle generously with toasted almonds

English Trifle
England

Let stand 24 hours in earthen dish in refrigerator before serving. Whip cream with a dash of vanilla if desired.

---

1 large can milk, chilled until icy
2 lemons, juice and grated rind

1 cup sugar
Drop of desired food coloring

Frozen Lemon Mist
Southern

Whip chilled milk until stiff. Add sugar and lemon juice and rind. Turn into a crumb lined pan and freeze.

---

6 eggs, separated
1 pound sugar
1 pound butter

1 pound flour
1 heaping teaspoon baking powder
Vanilla or almond extract to taste

Powdered Sugar Glaze

1 cup powdered sugar
1 teaspoon vanilla

2 tablespoons warm water or enough to make smooth paste

Butter Pound Cake
Southern

Cream butter and egg yolks until fluffy. Add sugar, flour and vanilla. Fold in egg whites, beaten stiff. Last add baking powder and mix thoroughly. Pour into a greased tube cake pan and bake for 1 hour at 325 degrees. Ice while hot with glaze.

¾ cup flour
½ teaspoon salt
½ teaspoon sugar

½ cup milk
1 egg
1 tablespoon oil

Timbale Shells
Southern

Mix all ingredients until smooth. Let stand for 30 minutes. Heat irons, wipe dry, dip into batter (being careful not to dip irons too deep) and fry in 2 inches of hot oil until brown. Remove from iron and roll in powdered sugar.

Leave cases plain if they are to be used for vegetables, etc..

---

1 cup flour
1 teaspoon baking powder
1 stick butter

1 cup sugar
1 cup milk
2 cups juicy sweetened blackberries, peaches, apples, etc.

Fruit Cobbler
Southern

Melt butter in baking pan. Combine flour, sugar, baking powder and milk. Pour over butter. Next spoon hot fruit and juice over batter. DO NOT STIR. Bake in 350 degree oven for 45 minutes.

Sprinkle cobbler with sugar during the last 10 minutes of baking.

Chocolate Fruit
South America

1-6 ounce package semi-sweet chocolate chips
1/4 cup half and half
1 teaspoon vanilla extract

Melt chocolate chips in double boiler, add half and half. Stir until hot, add vanilla. Cut up slices of bananas, fresh pears, apples, pineapple, seedless grapes and chop some nuts. Serve each person sliced fruit; a small cup of hot chocolate and nuts. Let each dip his fruit into chocolate and then into nuts. If chocolate is too thick, thin with hot milk or cream. A marvelous dessert!

Peach Crisp
Southern

4 cups peaches
¾ cup sugar
½ teaspoon cinnamon
1 cup flour
1 stick butter

Put peaches in pyrex baking dish. Sprinkle with half of the sugar. Blend remaining sugar, flour, cinnamon and butter until consistency of pastry. Sprinkle crumbly mixture over peaches. Bake for 35 minutes in 375° oven or until crispy. Serve with whipped cream.

Fudge Sauce (Hot)
Southern

½ cup butter
2¼ cups confectioners' sugar
2/3 cup evaporated milk
6 squares bitter chocolate

Mix all ingredients. Cook over hot water in double boiler for 30 minutes. DO NOT STIR. Beat smooth and serve.

"Tutti Fruiti"
Southern

1 large can Alberta peaches, chopped
1 large can pineapple cubes
1 large can crushed pineapple
½ cup sliced maraschino cherries
3 cups sugar
1 cup bourbon or rum

Drain juice from fruit. Add sugar and boil 5 minutes. Add fruit and chill. Stir in bourbon or rum and store in refrigerator.

Butter Scotch Sauce
Southern

butter scotch sauce

1/3 cup butter
1 cup brown sugar
2 tablespoons light corn syrup
1/3 cup heavy cream

Bring all to a boil, stir and cool.

Vanilla Sauce
Southern

1 cup light cream
¼ cup sugar
1 tablespoon vanilla
1 tablespoon cornstarch
¼ cup cold water

Heat to boiling point the cream, sugar and vanilla. Stir in cornstarch which has been dissolved in ¼ cup cold water. DO NOT overcook. Cook just until thick. Serve hot over pudding or cake.

Almond Coconut Squares
Southern

¼ pound almonds
Coconut, ¼ pound
Graham crackers, ¼ pound
Butter, ¼ pound

Melt butter and add to graham crackers. Mix with ground almonds and coconut. Make into roll and chill in refrigerator then slice. Serve with vanilla ice cream and cherry preserves.

Hot Water Pastry
Southern

½ cup lard or Crisco
½ cup boiling water
½ teaspoon salt
Enough flour to make stiff dough

Place Crisco in a measuring cup. Fill cup with hot water. Add salt; turn mixture into bowl and add flour, mixing lightly.

2½ cups sifted cake flour
½ teaspoon salt

⅔ cup shortening
About ½ cup ice water

Mix and sift together the flour and salt. Cut in shortening and add small amount of water at a time mixing lightly. Use only enough water to hold dough together. Be sure your dough is not crumbly or sticky. Chill and then put dough on lightly floured board and roll out to ⅛ inch thickness. Fit pastry loosely in pie pan. Prick with fork and bake in a 450° oven for 15 minutes. Make a two-crust 9 inch pie.

1½ cups flour
½ cup shortening
1 teaspoon baking powder
½ teaspoon salt

1 egg yolk, beaten
2 tablespoons sugar
4 tablespoons ice water

Sift dry ingredients together in a bowl. Mix egg yolk with ice water. Blend in with dry ingredients the shortening and make into dough with egg yolk, ice water mixture. Roll out to about ⅛ of an inch and line an 8 inch pie pan.

Mix 1½ cups graham cracker crumbs with ¼ to ½ cup melted butter and ¼ cup sugar. Cover the sides and bottom of 8 inch pie pan with this mixture. If you wish it sweeter use a little more sugar.

2½ cups flour
1 cup butter
½ cup powdered sugar
1 tsp vanilla

Mix all together, pat into pan & bake at 300° for 25 minutes.

Follow recipe for shortbread. Roll dough about ⅛ inch thick and cut with biscuit cutter. Prick half the biscuits with fork tines. Bake at 300 degrees about 15 minutes. When cool, spread pricked biscuit with jam. Place the unpricked biscuit on top and frost with decorator's icing, made by blending 1 cup sifted confectioner's sugar, ¼ teaspoon salt, and ½ teaspoon vanilla with enough milk or water to make a smooth paste.

4 egg yolks
¾ cup sugar
1 stick butter

1 cup canned milk
1 teaspoon vanilla

Beat together the egg yolks and sugar and place on stove. Melt butter in egg mixture. Stir constantly. Remove from stove as soon as butter melts. Add canned milk and vanilla. Pour into partially baked pie crust and bake for 15 minutes at 400° then reduce heat and bake until custard sets. Cover pie with meringue.

PIE CRUST:
1½ cups flour

½ cup mayonnaise
Juice of ½ orange

Blend ingredients and roll out.

Peanut Butter Pie
Africa

4 eggs
1 1/4 cup sugar
1/2 stick butter, melted

1 cup sour cream
1/2 cup peanut butter
1 Tbs. vanilla

Mix ingredients. Pour in unbaked pie shell. Bake 35 minutes at 350°.

Old Fashion Cream Pie
Southern

1 pint thin cream
2/3 cup sugar
3 egg whites

1/8 teaspoon nutmeg
1/2 teaspoon vanilla
1/4 teaspoon salt

Pour the cream over the sugar and mix thoroughly. Let stand while beating the egg whites stiff. Fold the egg whites, nutmeg, flavoring and salt into the cream and sugar mixture, mixing well. Pour into a pastry lined pie pan. Bake in a hot oven, 425°, for 10 minutes. Reduce heat to 325° and bake until filling is firm.

Coffee Carnival
Southern

1/4 cup tapioca (minute)
1/2 cup sugar
1/2 teaspoon salt
1 1/2 cups water

1/3 cup raisins
1 cup strong coffee
1 teaspoon vanilla
1 cup cream, whipped

Combine in saucepan and bring to a boil the first five ingredients, cooking over medium heat and stirring constantly. Remove from heat and add coffee and vanilla. Cool. Fold in whipped cream. Serve very cold.

Sweet Potato Pecan Pie
Southern

1 1/2 cups cooked mashed sweet potatoes
1/2 cup brown sugar
1 teaspoon ground ginger

1 teaspoon ground cinnamon
1/4 teaspoon salt
1 1/2 cups scalded milk
2 well beaten eggs

Beat all ingredients together. Pour in unbaked pie shell and bake for 20 minutes in 350° oven. Then sprinkle on topping and continue to bake until set; about 25 minutes longer.

TOPPING:
3/4 cup chopped pecans

1/2 stick butter
1/4 cup brown sugar

Mix until crumbly.

Brown Sugar Custard
Southern

2 cups brown sugar
1 cup nuts
2 tablespoons flour
1 teaspoon vanilla

2 cups cream or canned milk
4 eggs separated
2 tablespoons butter (melted)

Mix brown sugar, flour, cream, vanilla, egg yolks and nuts together. Add butter and mix thoroughly. Pour mixture into unbaked pie shell (9-inch) and bake for 10 minutes in a 400° oven then reduce heat to 300° and bake until pie is set. Make meringue, using the egg whites and 8 tablespoons sugar. Brown in oven.

Buttermilk Pie
Southern

4 eggs
2 cups sugar
2 tablespoons flour
2/3 cup buttermilk

1/2 cup margarine, melted
1 teaspoon vanilla
Pinch salt

Blend all ingredients together. Bake in large unbaked pie shell (or 2 small shells) at 325° until firm.

1 1/4 cups sugar
1 tablespoon cornstarch
1 1/ cups sweet milk (I use canned)
3 eggs, separated

2 tablespoons flour
2 tablespoons melted butter
Dash of salt
1 baked pie shell

Caramel Pie
United States

Caramelize 1/4 cup sugar in heavy skillet. Do not stir. While the sugar is caramelizing, combine sugar, flour and cornstarch with butter and milk. Blend in egg yolks. Cover and cook over low heat until thick. Add hot caramel sugar to custard. Stir until smooth and continue cooking until thick and creamy. Pour into prebaked pie shell. Top with meringue made with 3 egg whites and 6 tablespoons sugar. Brown in 300 degree oven.

1/2 cup melted butter
4 whole eggs
1/4 teaspoon salt
1 unbaked pie shell

1/3 cup cocoa
1 cup sugar
1 teaspoon vanilla

Chocolate Fudge Pie
Southern

Mix all ingredients quickly. Put in pie shell and bake in 350 degrees oven until firm, about 30 minutes. DO NOT OVERCOOK. This pie has a custard texture. Serve warm with ice cream.

---

1 large lemon (grated rind and juice)
1 cup sugar
½ cup milk
2 tablespoons cornstarch

2 tablespoons butter, melted
3 eggs separated
6 tablespoons sugar for meringue

Lemon Pie in Uncooked Pastry
United States

Mix together all ingredients except egg whites and 6 tablespoons sugar. Pour into an uncooked pie crust and bake. When nearly done make the meringue of the whites and 6 tablespoons of sugar. Brown in slow oven. Bake the pie for 10 minutes at 400° and then reduce heat at 300° and bake until pie is set. Top with meringue and brown in 300° oven.

---

2 eggs
½ cup sugar
½ teaspoon salt
2 tablespoons flour

¾ cup karo syrup
1 teaspoon vanilla
2 tablespoons melted butter
1 cup shredded coconut

Coconut Pie
French

Mix ingredients together in order given. Put in unbaked pie shell and bake for 45 minutes or until firm in a 350° oven.

To get the coconut meat from the shell easily, place the whole coconut uncracked in a 450° oven for 10 min. Remove from oven and tap gently all around the shell. The shell will fall away from the meat.

---

1 pint milk
3 egg yolks
½ cup sugar

Pinch salt
3 tablespoons cornstarch
1 teaspoon vanilla

Banana Cream Pie
Southern

Blend ingredients and cook in double boiler until thick. Let cool. Make layers of bananas and cooled custard. Cover with layer of sweetened whipped cream.

Black Walnut Pie
Southern

2 eggs, beaten
1 cup dark corn syrup
Scant ⅛ teaspoon salt
1 teaspoon vanilla

1 cup sugar
2 tablespoons melted butter
1 cup walnuts

Combine all ingredients. Pour filling into uncooked pie shell and bake in 350° oven until firm, about 50 minutes. For a pie not quite so sweet use ¾ cup syrup and ½ cup white sugar. Bake as usual.

Pecan Pie
Southern

1 cup chopped pecans
1 cup Karo syrup
½ cup sugar
½ teaspoon salt

3 tablespoons melted margarine
1 teaspoon vanilla
3 eggs
1 unbaked pie crust

Beat eggs slightly. Add vanilla, margarine, salt, sugar, Karo syrup. Blend well. Add chopped pecans. Pour in pie crust. Bake for 12 minutes in a 375 degree oven; reduce heat to 325° and continue baking until pie is set.

Chess Pie
Southern

1 cup sugar
½ cup butter
3 eggs
1½ teaspoons vinegar

1 teaspoon vanilla flavoring
1 teaspoon almond flavoring
½ cup ground almonds (optional) or 1 Tbs. cornmeal

Cream butter; add sugar gradually and blend thoroughly. Add eggs and beat well. Stir in vanilla and almond flavoring. Sprinkle unbaked pie shell with ground almonds then pour in the above mixture and bake in 400° oven for 12 minutes. Reduce heat to 350° and bake for 15 minutes longer until done.

Chocolate Chess Pie
Southern

3 eggs
½ cup butter
3 tablespoons cocoa (heaping)

1 tablespoon vanilla
1¼ cup sugar
½ cup cream (sour or sweet)

Beat all together quickly. Pour into unbaked pie crust. Bake 35 minutes at 350 degrees.

Fresh Strawberry Pie
Southern

1 cup sugar
1 cup water
2 heaping tablespoons cornstarch

Red food coloring
½ teaspoon lemon juice

Cook sugar, water and cornstarch until thick. Remove from heat and add lemon juice and food coloring. Line baked pie shell with fresh whole strawberries and cover with cooked mixture. Serve with whipped cream.

Layered Mocha Pie
United States

½ cup coffee
½ cup evaporated milk
1 cup sugar
¼ teaspoon salt

½ teaspoon rum flavoring
2 squares grated chocolate
4 eggs separated

Mix all ingredients. Pour in pie shell and bake in a 350° oven until done, approximately 45 minutes. Top with meringue.

2 tablespoons tapioca
1 tablespoon sifted flour
1 cup sugar
⅛ teaspoon salt
½ cup cherry juice drained

from No. 2 can sour pitted
cherries
1 No. 2 can sour pitted cherries
¼ teaspoon almond extract
½ teaspoon red food coloring
(if desired)

**Cherry Pie
Deluxe**
Southern

Mix tapioca, flour and sugar. Stir in cherry juice, salt, cherries, almond extract and coloring. Let stand for 15 minutes. Pour in unbaked pie shell. Make lattice top with strips of pastry. Brush with butter and bake for 10 minutes in a 400° oven then reduce heat to 350° and bake until pie is set.

---

3 eggs
1 cup sugar
1 tablespoon butter, melted

1½ lemons (juiced)
1 tablespoon water
1 heaping tablespoon corn meal

**Original
Jefferson
Davis
Custard**
Southern

Beat eggs and add sugar gradually, blending until fluffy. Add butter, lemon juice, water and corn meal. Beat until smooth. Pour into unbaked pie shell and bake for 35 minutes in a 350° oven until firm.

1¼ cups brazil nuts, ground   3 tablespoons sugar

Combine ground nuts and sugar. Press into pie pan and bake in 400° oven for about 8 minutes or until lightly browned.

PIE FILLING:
1 envelope plain gelatin
¼ cup water
3 egg yolks
¼ cup sugar
⅛ teaspoon salt

1½ cups scalded milk
½ cup thinly sliced candied
cherries
2 tablespoons rum
3 egg whites
¼ cup sugar

**Brazil Nut
Crust Pie**
Carribean

Soak gelatin in water. Beat egg yolks. Add sugar, salt and gradually stir in scalded milk. Cook in double boiler over very hot water until it coats the spoon. Remove and stir in gelatin. Chill custard until it holds its shape when dropped from spoon. Beat smooth. Add sliced cherries and rum. Now beat the egg whites and add ¼ cup sugar. Fold into custard. Pour into pie shell. Place in refrigerator and chill several hours. Top with whipped cream and sliced Brazil nuts.

½ cup sugar
4 tablespoons flour
⅛ teaspoon salt
1 cup milk
1 sq. chocolate (melted)

6 marshmallows
1 tablespoon butter
1 baked pie shell
Sweetened whipped cream
Flavored with vanilla

**Swiss
Chocolate Pie**
International

Blend sugar, flour and salt; stir in milk until smooth. Cook over low heat, stirring constantly until thick. Add melted chocolate and marshmallows and butter. Stir until dissolved then cool. Pour in baked pie shell, top with whipped cream. Chill in refrigerator until serving time.

⅓ cup sugar
½ cup flour
¼ teaspoon salt
3 cups milk
1 cup shredded coconut

2 slightly beaten egg yolks
2 teaspoons vanilla
1 tablespoon butter
1 baked 9-inch pie shell

Coconut Pie Deluxe
Southern

Combine sugar, flour and salt in top of double boiler. Add milk gradually, stirring until smooth. Add ¾ cup coconut and cook over rapidly boiling water for 15 minutes stirring until stiff. Mix small amount of mixture with egg yolks and then add to the cream mixture and cook 2 minutes longer. Remove from heat. Add vanilla and butter. Cool. Put in pie shell and sprinkle with coconut. Top with meringue.

MERINGUE:
2 egg whites
½ cup sugar
⅛ teaspoon salt

3 tablespoons water
½ teaspoon vanilla
½ cup shredded coconut

Place egg whites, sugar, salt and water in double boiler. Beat with electric beater until thoroughly mixed. Place over rapidly boiling water and beat for 1 minute. Remove from heat and continue beating until mixture forms peaks. Add flavoring. Pile lightly on filling. Sprinkle with coconut, plain or toasted.

---

3 egg whites
1 cup sugar
¼ teaspoon baking powder
Pinch salt

20 chopped dates
½ cup nuts chopped
12 soda crackers rolled fine

Macaroon Pie
Southern

Beat egg whites until stiff. Add sugar, baking powder and salt gradually. Mix in other ingredients. Pour in greased pie pan and cook in 350° oven for 20 minutes. Do not over bake. Wonderful hot or cold. Whipped cream or ice cream topping can be used, but is good plain.

---

1 cup sugar
1 cup thick sour cream
1 cup raisins (dusted with

flour)
1 teaspoon vanilla

Sour Cream Pie
Southern

Mix all ingredients. Put in unbaked pie shell. Cover with top crust and bake in a 350° oven for 45 minutes to 1 hour until nice and brown.

---

1 cup sugar
2 rounded tablespoons flour
1 cup milk
3 tablespoons cocoa
3 eggs, separated

1 tablespoon butter
1 teaspoon vanilla
⅛ teaspoon salt
1 baked pie shell

Chocolate Cream Pie
Southern

Mix sugar, cocoa, flour and salt. Add ½ of milk and 1 egg yolk; beat well. Add other egg yolks and beat thoroughly then add rest of milk. Cook until thick and be sure to stir constantly. Cool and put in baked pie shell. Make meringue out of the 3 egg whites, beaten until fluffy; then add 6 tablespoons sugar, beating until it stands in peaks.

Stir 1 tablespoon flour into 4 tablespoons melted butter. Add ½ tablespoon nutmeg, 1 cup sugar, ¾ cup orange juice and mix all together. Chop 5 medium winesap apples and place on pastry. Pour above ingredients over apples. Strip top with pastry. Bake 15 minutes in 450° oven then reduce heat to 300° and bake 25-30 minutes.

Apple Pie
Southern

---

3 eggs, separated
1 cup sugar
3 tablespoons flour, heaping

1 can crushed pineapple
1 tablespoon butter
Baked pie shell

Blend sugar, flour, and stir in pineapple. Cook in saucepan over low heat until stiff. And egg yolks, beaten well, and butter. Cook a few minutes longer. Cool. Put cooled filling in baked pie shell and top with meringue. Brown in oven.

Pineapple Pie
United States

---

1 teaspoon gelatin
½ cup lime juice
2 eggs
1 tablespoon sugar

1 can sweetened condensed milk
Whipping cream
Pie shell

Dissolve gelatin in lime juice. Beat egg yolks until lemon colored. Add ½ tablespoon sugar (the gelatin and lime juice)* and sweetened condensed milk and beat thoroughly. Fold in egg whites beaten stiff with ½ tablespoon sugar, and pour the mixture into a baked pie shell. When the filling is set, top with whipped cream. *Be sure and melt over hot water.

Key West Lime Pie
Southern

¼ cup sugar
Dash salt
½ teaspoon almond extract

½ teaspoon vanilla
1¼ cups scalded milk
3 egg whites

Add sugar, salt, almond and vanilla extract to scalded milk. Pour over slightly beaten egg whites, stirring constantly. Pour in custard cups; place in a pan of hot water and bake in a 350° oven for 25 minutes or until tip of inserted knife comes out clean.

Egg White Custard
Southern

---

1 unbaked pie crust
3 egg whites, stiffly beaten
½ cup sugar
½ teaspoon vanilla

Coconut
Whipped cream
Toasted pecans

Mix until fluffy, egg whites, sugar and vanilla. Put mixture in pie shell. Sprinkle with coconut. Bake in 300° oven for 30 minutes. Cool. Top with whipped cream and toasted pecans. Store in refrigerator until ready to use.

Angel Food Pie
United States

---

1 cup sugar
¼ cup flour
2 squares or 4 heaping tablespoons cocoa

½ cup melted butter
2 whole eggs
1 teaspoon vanilla

Mix all together. Grease pyrex baking plate with butter. Pour in mixture. Bake at 325° for 25-30 minutes. Cool. Cut in wedges. Serve topped with ice cream.

Fudge Pie Cake
United States

6 eggs yolks
1 tablespoon gelatin
1 pint heavy cream
Bitter chocolate

1 cup sugar
1/4 cup water
1/2 cup rum
Graham cracker pie crust

Rum Cream Pie
Southern

Beat the egg yolks and the cup of sugar until light. Measure the water in a cup and soak the gelatin. Put the cup in a pan of boiling water and sitr until the gelatin is dissolved. Pour into egg mixture, beating briskly. Let cool. Whip cream until stiff, fold in egg mixture. Add 1/2 cup rum. Pour into graham cracker crust, and place in refrigerator to set. Before serving, grate bitter chocolate over the top of the pie. It's rich as can be and delicious.

3 cups scalded milk
½ cup sugar
¼ teaspoon salt
1 teaspoon vanilla
3 eggs

1 12-ounce package vanilla wafers
1 package gelatin (plain) (dissolved in 2 tablespoons cold water)

Banana Pudding
Southern

Beat egg yolks and sugar until creamy. Add salt and vanilla. Mix with hot milk. Cook until it coats spoon. Dissolve gelatin mixture in custard. Cool. Pour over bananas and vanilla wafers placed in layers in pyrex dish. Top with meringue, made with egg whites and ½ cup sugar. Brown in oven.

½ cup butter
1 cup boiling water
1 cup enriched flour

¼ teaspoon salt
4 eggs

Cream Puffs
International

Melt butter in water. Add flour and salt all at once. Stir vigorously. Cook, stirring constantly until mixture forms ball that doesn't separate. Remove from heat and cool slightly. Add eggs, one at a time beating vigorously after each addition until mixture is smooth. Drop from teaspoon 2 inches apart onto greased baking sheet. Bake for 15 minutes at 450°. Reduce heat to 325° and bake for 25 minutes longer. When cool fill with sweetened whipped cream.

3 eggs
1 teaspoon sugar
¼ teaspoon salt
1 cup heavy cream

¾ cups flour
Powdered sugar
Cinnamon

Swiss Fried Cakes
Switzerland

Beat eggs well and add the sugar and salt. Then stir in the cream. Gradually sift in the flour, using only enough to make a stiff dough. Place dough on floured board and roll very thin. Cut in strips or squares and fry in hot deep fat until brown. Roll in powdered sugar and cinnamon while hot.

3 tablespoons butter
6 tablespoons confectioners sugar
⅔ cup flour

Few grains salt
3 tablespoons milk
½ teaspoon vanilla

Wafer Cups
Southern

Cream butter and add sugar. Cream thoroughly. Mix flour and salt and add to first mixture alternately with milk. Add vanilla. Bake in a 325° oven for 12 minutes. Shape by placing on baking tin and smoothing out. While hot after baking shape over tea cup and let cool.

1 quart milk
½ cup sugar
3 to 5 eggs
1 teaspoon flour

Pinch salt
½ teaspoon lemon extract
½ teaspoon vanilla extract
¼ teaspoon almond extract

Boiled Custard Deluxe
Southern

Put ¾ quart of milk on to scald. Save 3 egg whites. Beat egg yolks and sugar and flour and ¼ of milk. Add to scalding milk. Cook until it coats spoon over low heat. Beat egg whites. After custard has cooled add flavorings and fold in egg whites. Stir until well blended. This is excellent.

1½ pound young rhubarb
¾ to 1 cup sugar
½ cup boiling water
3 teaspoons gelatin

1½ tablespoons cold water
½ cup heavy cream, whipped
Grated rind of ½ orange

Jellied Rhubarb Mold
Europe

Wash rhubarb. Dice and place in sauce pan with the sugar and water. Cover and cook 15 minutes. Drain off hot juice and add to gelatin (softened in water). Stir well and pour over rhubarb. Let stand in refrigerator until firm. Serve with orange flavored whipped cream.

---

4 egg whites
1 cup fine granulated sugar

½ teaspoon vanilla
Food coloring

Meringues
French

Beat egg whites until stiff. Add gradually 2/3 cups sugar. Fold in 1/3 cup sugar and vanilla. Add food coloring and shape with spoon on cookie sheet covered with wax paper. Bake in a slow oven 275° for 30 to 35 minutes. Top with ice cream, whipping cream, etc.

1¼ sticks butter
¼ cup sugar
1½ cups flour

Jelly
Powdered sugar icing

Real Short Cakes
Scotland

Cream butter, sugar and flour. Roll out to ¼ inch thickness on lightly floured board. Cut out in small rounds. Bake in a 300° oven until pale brown. While still hot place 2 rounds together with jelly. Ice with plain powdered sugar icing. Top with pecan half. Delicious with tea.

---

16 vanilla wafers
3 eggs, separated
1 cup chopped nuts
1 cup powdered sugar

¼ pound butter
1½ squares bitter chocolate
½ teaspoon vanilla

English Toffee Squares
International

Roll wafers and line square pan with ½ of the crumbs. Beat egg yolks, cup nuts, powdered sugar, butter, chocolate and vanilla until creamy. Add stiffly beaten egg whites, folding gently. Pour mixture into pan. Top with rest of crumbs. Chill for 2 hours and serve with whipped cream.

¾ cup cake flour
¾ teaspoon baking powder
¼ teaspoon salt
4 eggs

¾ cup sugar
1 teaspoon vanilla extract
1 cup jelly

Jelly Roll
International

Start oven at 400°. Grease a 15x10x1½ inch jelly roll pan. Fit with layer of greased wax paper. Sift flour. Beat eggs, baking powder and salt until fluffy. Add sugar gradually and beat until mixture is smooth. Fold in flour and vanilla. Bake for 13 minutes. Roll up cake—let cool—spread with jelly.

2 cups powdered sugar
2 cups shortening

Cream Whip Filling for Jelly Rolls and Cakes
International

Beat together powdered sugar and shortening for 8 minutes. In the top of a double boiler cook and stir constantly for 2 minutes a mixture of 1 cup sugar, 4 egg whites, 1 teaspoon salt and 1 teaspoon vanilla. Cool until lukewarm and beat until peaks form. Now to the whipped sugar and shortening add whipped egg mixture in 3 parts, beating well after each addition. After adding last amount of eggs, beat 8 minutes. Cover and use as needed. Will not get sugary. Delicious for coconut cakes, too.

Sift together and set aside:
6 tablespoons cocoa
1/2 cup flour
1/3 teaspoon baking powder
1/4 teaspoon salt
1/4 teaspoon baking soda
2 tablespoons sugar

Beat until very light and fluffy:
4 eggs at room temperature
3/4 cup granulated sugar
1 teaspoon vanilla

Fold dry ingredients into whipped eggs and sugar; adding 3 tablespoons cold water to help blend. Turn into a 15 x 10 x 1-inch baking sheet lined with waxed paper that has been well-greased.

Chocolate Cream Roll
International

Bake in preheated oven of 400 degrees for 15 minutes or until firm to touch. Turn cake onto muslin cloth. Remove paper and roll-up jellyroll fashion, leaving cloth on cake. Cool. Carefully unroll and remove cloth. Spread with sweetened whipped cream (1 cup whipped cream, 1/3 cup powdered sugar, vanilla). Carefully roll cake back up and ice with Chocolate Water Glaze:

1/2 cup powdered sugar
1 tablespoon cocoa
1 to 2 tablespoons hot water

Mix until smooth and dribble over cake. Decorate with marashino cherries and pecans if desired.

slices bread
Cream 1 cup powdered sugar
  with 6 tablespoons butter
½ cups milk

2 eggs
⅔ cup sugar
½ teaspoon nutmeg

Spread sugar and butter mixture on 4 slices of bread and cut each slice into 4 pieces. Place in greased baking dish. Pour remaining ingredients mixed over the bread and bake in a 350° oven for 30 minutes.
When pudding is done serve with whipped cream.

cup sugar
eggs
tablespoons milk
tablespoons flour

1 teaspoon baking powder
1 cup chopped nuts
1 cup chopped dates

Separate yolks from whites of eggs. Beat yolks until light and stir in sugar and milk. Sift flour and baking powder together and add to mixture. Then add dates, nuts and stiffly beaten egg whites. Bake in a well greased square pan in a 350° oven for 30 minutes. Serve cold with whipped cream.

cups of sliced apples
cup sugar
rounded tablespoon flour

1 pinch salt
¼-½ teaspoon cinnamon

Mix and put in baking pan. Top with the following ingredients.

TOPPING:
¼ cup oatmeal, uncooked
¼ cup flour
¼ cup brown sugar

¼ teaspoon soda
¼ teaspoon baking powder
⅓ cup melted butter

Mix well and pat over apple mixture. Bake in a 350° oven for approximately 30 minutes. Serve with ice cream or whipped cream or plain.

squares chocolate
⅓ cup condensed milk
egg, separated
teaspoon ginger

1 teaspoon vanilla
Lady fingers
Whipped cream

Melt chocolate in pan. Add condensed milk and cook slowly until thick. Add beaten egg yolk, ginger, vanilla and cook a few minutes longer. Fold in egg whites. Alternate layers of chocolate mixture with lady fingers. Place in refrigerator to cool. Top with whipping cream and serve.

CHEESE CAKE:
1¼ pounds cream cheese
⅞ cup sugar
1½ tablespoons flour

¾ teaspoon grated orange and
  lemon rind
⅛ teaspoon vanilla
3 eggs
⅛ cup heavy cream

Blend all ingredients until smooth. Pour into graham cracker lined pan. Bake at 350° for 1 hour until set. Let cool in pan.

Quick Fudge Pudding
Southern

1 cup flour
2 teaspoons baking powder
½ teaspoon salt
¾ cup granulated sugar
2 tablespoons cocoa

TOPPING
¾ cup brown sugar

½ cup milk
1 teaspoon vanilla
2 tablespoons melted
   shortening
¾ cup chopped walnuts

¼ cup cocoa
1¾ cups hot water

Sift together flour, baking powder, salt, granulated sug
and cocoa. Add milk, vanilla and shortening; mix unt
smooth. Add nut meats. Pour into greased 8 inch square
Bake in moderate oven, 350°, approximately 40-50 minute

Charlotte Russe
Southern

1½ dozen lady fingers
2 envelopes plain gelatin
½ cup cold water
2 cups milk

6 egg yolks
1 cup sugar
Vanilla to taste
2 cups heavy cream

Line mold with lady fingers. Soften gelatin in cold wate
Make custard out of milk, egg yolks and sugar. Cook unt
it thickens. Stir in gelatin. Let cool. Fold in whipped crea
and vanilla. Pour in mold. Let chill overnight in refrigerato

Butterscotch Ice Box Cookie Cake
Southern

1 package butterscotch pudding
   mix
1 envelope unflavored gelatin

1¾ cups cold water
1 pint vanilla ice cream
38 snack size coconut bars

Combine pudding mix, gelatin and cold water. Cook ac
cording to directions on package. Cool slightly, stirring onc
or twice. Add ice cream and stir until it is melted. Chill unt
slightly thickened. Arrange 6 cookies in bottom of 9x5 inc
loaf pan. Spoon 1/3 of mixture over cookies; then place 1
cookies on top of pudding and 4 cookies against long side
of pan. Continue layering pudding and cookies, making
layers of each. Chill until firm—at least for one hour.

Jello Creme Squares
Southern

1 package vanilla wafers
   (crumbs)
1 tall can evaporated milk
   (chilled and whipped)
2 lemons (juiced)
1 cup sugar

1 package lemon jello
1 cup hot water
1 small can pineapple
1 small bottle maraschino che
   ries
½ cup chopped pecans

Line refrigerator dish with ½ of wafer crumbs. Whip mil
until stiff, then add lemon juice and sugar beating unt
fluffy. Have jello dissolved in hot water and chilled unt
ready to congeal. Beat the jello into milk mixture. Fold i
pineapple, cherries and pecans. Place on top of vanilla wafe
crumbs. Top with remainder of crumbs. Chill until firn
Cut in squares to serve.

Turkish Delights
Asia

1 package lemon gelatin
1 cup hot water
Juice of 1 orange
Juice of 1 lemon

½ cup chopped nutmeats
Powdered sugar
Toothpicks

Dissolve gelatin in hot water. Add rest of ingredients ex
cept powdered sugar. When firm cut in tiny squares. Rol
in powdered sugar. Serve with toothpicks. (Nice for teas)

packages orange jello
cups hot water
small can crushed pineapple
   (drained)
No. 2 can sliced peaches
   (drained)
bananas (sliced)

20 marshmallows cut in fourths
1 small bottle of maraschino
   cherries
1 pint whipping cream
1 small sponge or angel food
   cake (round)

Fruit Ice Box Cake
Southern

Cut cake into thin layers. Dissolve jello in hot water. Add 2 cups drained juice from fruits. Add fruits, and marshmallows. When cool fold in whipped cream. Alternate layers of cake and jello mixture in large tube cake pan. Let set overnight in refrigerator. Slice and serve with whipped cream.

½ cups flour
½ cups sugar
teaspoons baking powder
teaspoon salt
½ cup Wesson oil
unbeaten egg yolks

Grated rind of 2 oranges
Juice of 2 oranges and enough
   water to make ¾ cups liquid
1 cup egg whites
½ teaspoon cream tartar

Orange Chiffon Cake
Southern

Sift together first four ingredients. Add next four ingredients and beat 1 minute. Fold in egg whites beaten with ½ teaspoon cream tartar. Bake in tube cake pan at 325° for 70 minutes.

---

cup shortening
¾ cups sugar
eggs beaten
½ teapsoons soda
teaspoon salt
cup buttermilk

3 cups flour
1 tablespoon orange juice
1 tablespoon orange rind
1 package dates rolled in flour
1 cup pecans

Danish Pudding Cake
Danish

Cream shortening and sugar. Add beaten eggs, orange juice and rind. Sift dry ingredients together and add alternately with buttermilk. Fold in dates and pecans. Pour into large angel food pan and bake in a 350° oven for about 1 hour and 20 minutes. Soon as taken from oven pour sauce over pudding. Let cool before removing cake from pan.

SAUCE:

grated orange rind rubbed into 1 cup sugar

1 cup orange juice

Mix all ingredients and stir until dissolved.

---

eggs
cup Wesson oil
½ cups sugar
cups flour
teaspoon soda
teaspoon cinnamon
teaspoon nutmeg

1 teaspoon allspice
1 teaspoon salt
1 cup buttermilk
1 cup prunes, cooked and cut
1 teaspoon vanilla
1 cup nuts

Prune Cake
Southern

Blend sugar and oil. Add eggs. Blend well. Add sifted dry ingredients and milk alternately. Add vanilla, nuts, and prunes. Bake in low cake pan, greased or 2 8x8x2 inch pans in 300° oven until done. Leave cake in pan until ready to serve.

Chocolate Cake
International

2 eggs
1¾ cups sugar
2 cups flour, sifted
1 teaspoon baking soda
½ teaspoon salt

½ cup melted butter
¾ cup milk
¼ cup vinegar
1 teaspoon vanilla
3 squares chocolate

Cream eggs and sugar until light. Add dry ingredients alternately with butter, milk and vinegar mixing until smooth. Add vanilla and melted chocolate. Bake in 350° oven for 30 minutes.

Tomato Soup Cake
Southern

1 can tomato soup
½ cup margarine
1 teaspoon soda
⅛ teaspoon salt
1 teaspoon nutmeg

2 cups cake flour
1 cup brown sugar
1 teaspoon cinnamon
2 teaspoons baking powder
½ teaspoon cloves

Add melted butter to soup. Add sugar and rest of ingredients. Mix well. Pour into rectangular pan and bake for 45 minutes at 325°. Top with icing made from 1½ cups powdered sugar, 1 package cream cheese and 1 teaspoon vanilla.

Angel Food Cake
Southern

12 egg whites
1 rounded teaspoon cream of tartar
1 cup powdered sugar
1 cup granulated sugar

1 cup cake flour
½ teaspoon vanilla
½ teaspoon orange flavoring
¼ teaspoon almond flavoring

Add cream of tartar to egg whites and beat until a stiff moist foam (no longer). Sift flour, sugar and add slowly to whites. Fold gently after each addition. Then fold in flavorings. Bake in ungreased tube pan at 300° for one hour. Invert pan to cool.

The secret in making light, moist angel food cakes depends on beating the egg whites until they stand in peaks. They should be soft and moist looking—If you beat them until they are stiff and dry—shame on you. . . . Always fold in the dry ingredients carefully.

Hot Milk Cake
Southern

2 well-beaten eggs
1 cup sugar
1 cup flour
⅛ teaspoon salt

1 teaspoon baking powder
½ cup hot milk
1 tablespoon butter

Beat eggs light and thick. Slowly add sugar and beat with a spoon for 5 minutes or with mixer for 2½ minutes. Sift flour, salt and baking powder. Fold into egg and sugar mixture all at one time. (Work quickly. No puttering around). Melt butter in hot milk and add all at once. The folding in of the flour and milk should take only 60 seconds. Bake in 8 inch square pan in moderate oven at 360° for 30 minutes.

1 cup eggs (4 or 5 eggs)
1 cup butter or margarine
1 teaspoon vanilla
1/2 teaspoon baking powder

1 cup sifted, powdered sugar
2 cups sifted cornstarch
1/2 teaspoon vanilla
1/4 to 1/2 cup powdered sugar

Cornstarch Cake
Egypt

Beat eggs thoroughly; then beat in cup of powdered sugar; then blend in butter. Continue beating, gradually adding conrstarch. Beat in vanilla and baking powder. Bake in greased 8 x 8 x 2-inch pan at 375⁰ for 25 to 30 minutes. Sprinkle with powdered sugar as soon as taken from oven.

4 cups sour cream
  (Extra thick commercial)

1/3 cup dark brown sugar
1/4 cup Grand Marnier or Curacao

Faculous Sour Cream Dip
(For Fresh Strawberries)
International

Mix all together very quickly. Serve with fresh strawberries. *Do not over mix.

1 pound dates
4 slices crystalized pineapple
¼ pound crystalized cherries
⅛ pound crystalized citron
⅛ pound crystalized orange peel

1 cup pecans
1 can southern style coconut
1 can Eagle Brand sweetened condensed milk
Pinch of salt

Caramel Fruit Cake
Southern

Chop fruits, not too fine. Thoroughly mix all ingredients with hands. Line 8 inch tube pan (sides and bottom) with heavy brown paper, well greased. Firmly pack with fruit cake mixture, using hands to press well into pan. Bake for 1 hour in a 300° oven. Reduce heat to 250° and bake 1 hour longer or until light brown. Remove from pan while still warm. Wrap in wax paper and store in refrigerator for 1 week before cutting. Keeps indefinitely in refrigerator. Slice paper thin.

½ pound vanilla wafers
1½ cup confectioners sugar
½ cup butter
2 eggs

1 small can crushed pineapple
½ pint whipping cream
1 cup nuts

Pineapple Ice Box Cake
International

Crush vanilla wafers until fine. Put half of them in pyrex dish. Beat butter and powdered sugar until smooth. Add eggs and beat vigorously until creamy. Pour on top of vanilla wafers. Whip cream, fold in pineapple and nuts for top layer. Sprinkle with remaining vanilla wafer crumbs and place in refrigerator for two hours. Serve with additional whipped cream.

¾ cup butter
2 cups sugar
2½ cups cake flour
2½ teaspoons baking powder

⅛ teaspoon salt
1 cup milk
5 egg whites
1 teaspoon vanilla

White Cake
International

Cream butter and sugar until fluffy. Sift dry ingredients together and add alternately with milk. (Always add flour mixture first to creamed mixture.) Fold in egg whites which have been beaten until they are frothy. (Do not over beat. They should stand in moist peaks). Fold in vanilla. Pour into 2 well-greased cake pans lined with white paper. Bake in 350° oven for 25 to 30 minutes or until done. Let cool in pan.

Coconut Marshmallow Cake
Southern

1½ sticks butter
1 cup sugar
4 eggs, reserving whites of 2
　for icing
2 cups cake flour, sifted

½ teaspoon salt
2 teaspoons baking powder
½ cup milk
1 teaspoon vanilla

Cream sugar and butter, then add eggs one at a time. Keep the whites of two of them for the icing. Sift flour, salt and baking powder together. Add to mixture alternately with milk. Mix well and add vanilla. Pour into 2 9-inch round layer cake pans which have been lined with paper well greased. Bake in 350° oven for 30 minutes or until done.

Marshmallow Frosting
Southern

1 cup sugar
½ cup boiling water
¼ teaspoon vinegar

2 egg whites, stiffly beaten
10 marshmallows
1 cup fresh grated coconut

Place sugar, vinegar and boiling water in a saucepan and stir until the sugar is dissolved. Place on fire and cook until mixture forms a soft ball in cold water. Pour over stiffly beaten egg whites, beating constantly. Then add broken marshmallows and beat until dissolved. Ice Cake and sprinkle with coconut.

Chocolate Fudge Icing
Southern

2 cups sugar
⅔ cup water
1 stick butter

⅓ cup flour
½ cup cocoa
Vanilla

Cook sugar, cocoa and water to a soft ball stage. Cream butter and flour and add to syrup. Add vanilla and beat until creamy.

One Minute Caramel Icing
Southern

1 cup brown sugar
2 tablespoons butter
1 tablespoon flour

3 tablespoons cream
Pinch salt
1 teaspoon vanilla

Bring all ingredients to a boil except vanilla. Stir. Boil 1 minute. Add vanilla. Remove from stove and beat until it begins to thicken. Spread on cake. Covers 1 layer.

Coffee Butter Frosting
Southern

½ cup butter
3 cups confectioners sugar,
　sifted

1 teaspoon vanilla
3 tablespoons cocoa
4 tablespoons cold strong coffee

Cream butter and add remaining ingredients. Beat until creamy and smooth. Spread on cooled cake.

Ice Cream Bars
Southern

Cut ice cream in sticks. Insert wooden skewer in end. Dip in melted mixture of 6 ounces semi sweet chocolate pieces, 1 cup chopped peanuts and 1/4 cup butter. Allow to harden in freezer.

4 heaping tablespoons flour
1 cup milk
¾ cup shortening (Crisco or margarine)
¾ cup sugar
1 teaspoon flavoring
1½ cups powdered sugar (optional)

Italian Bakers Icing
Italy

Blend flour and milk. Cook over low heat until it forms a ball of dough. Let ball cool. When cool, put in mixing bowl and beat until fluffy. Add alternately to the dough mixture the sugar and shortening, continuing to beat until tripled in bulk. Add flavoring. The more you beat the nicer the icing. This makes a soft icing. If you desire to have your icing crust over add powdered sugar to the mixture just before spreading on cake.

1 teaspoon plain gelatin
4 teaspoons cold water
1 cup whipping cream
¼ cup confectioners sugar
½ teaspoon vanilla

Whipped Cream Icing
International

Let gelatin and water mixture stand until thick. Then melt gelatin-water mixture over steam. Let cool. Whip cream until medium stiff. Pour in gelatin all at once. Continue beating. Add confectioners sugar and vanilla. Spread on cake and let icing set.

¾ cup sugar
2 tablespoons flour
⅛ teaspoon salt
2 eggs, slightly beaten
1 large can crushed pineapple
3 tablespoons lemon juice
½ pint whipping cream
1 baked angel cake (in stem pan)

Soft Pineapple Frosting
Southern

Mix sugar, flour, salt. Add eggs, crushed pineapple, lemon juice and mix all thoroughly. Cook slowly until thick—about 15 minutes. Remove from heat and cool. May be stored in refrigerator overnight. Whip cream, and fold in pineapple mixture. Cut cake in 3 layers. Top each layer with filling and frost outside of cake with same. Garnish with toasted almonds.

1 teaspoon plain gelatin
⅔ cup cold water
8 cups powdered sugar
1 egg white
1 tablespoon white corn syrup
Tint with food coloring if desired

Petit Fours Decorating Icing
French

Dissolve gelatin in cold water in top of double boiler. Add rest of ingredients. Stir until blended. Place over hot water and heat to 110 degrees (this is warm to touch). Dip frozen cake squares in glaze and allow to dry.

⅓ cup egg whites
1 pound confectioners sugar
¼ teaspoon cream tartar

Royal Icing
(Decorating-Powdered Sugar)
Southern

Add ½ of sugar to egg whites and beat for 5 minutes. Add cream of tartar and rest of sugar ½ cup at a time, continually beating.

Butter Cream Icing (Professional)

2 boxes (2 pounds) powdered
  sugar
½ cup Crisco or butter
1 teaspoon vanilla or almond
  extract
⅓ to ½ cup cream

Mix in mixer. Add cream gradually to make right consistency to spread and decorate.

Decorative Icing (Boiled)
Southern

4 egg whites
2 cups sugar
3 ounces water

¼ teaspoon cream of tartar
1 teaspoon vanilla
½ teaspoon orange flavoring

Boil sugar and water to 232°. Pour while hot over stiffly beaten egg whites continually beating whites. When all syrup has been added to whites add cream of tartar and flavorings. Beat well into egg mixture.

Grape Sherbet
United States

1 cup sugar
2 cups hot water
1 cup canned crushed pineapple
Juice of 3 lemons

1 cup of bottled grape juice
1 can sweetened condensed
  milk

Dissolve sugar in hot water. Stir in rest of ingredients. Freeze, stirring often. Makes 1½ quarts.

Lime Sherbet
United States

1 package lime jello
1 cup hot water
½ cup sugar
2 cups milk

1 cup cream
¼ cup lemon juice
1 teaspoon grated lemon rind

Dissolve gelatin in hot water. Add remaining ingredients and mix thoroughly. Freeze in refrigerator until firm. Break into chunks and beat smooth. Return to freezing compartment until firm, or freeze in old-fashioned freezer. Makes 1½ quarts. Any flavored jello may be used.

Pineapple Buttermilk Sherbet
Southern

4 cups buttermilk
2 cups sugar
2 small cans crushed pineapple

2 teaspoons vanilla
2 egg whites (beaten fluffy)

Dissolve sugar in buttermilk. Stir in crushed pineapple and add vanilla. Fold in egg whites. Freeze, using 3 parts ice to 1 part salt. Makes 2 quarts.

Peppermint Ice Cream
United States

2 cups milk
2 cups heavy cream
½ pound peppermint stick
  candy

1 package plain gelatin
¼ cup water

Heat milk and crushed candy and stir until melted. Combine milk-candy mixture with cream. Stir in gelatin which has been dissolved in water. Freeze in hand freezer.

1 cup mashed avocado pulp
½ cup pineapple juice
½ cup orange juice
½ cup lemon juice

1¼ cups sugar
1 cup skimmed milk
¼ teaspoon salt

Avocado Milk Sherbet
South America

Dissolve sugar in milk by heating to lukewarm. Add the avocado plup and fruit juices. Mix smooth. Freeze in hand freezer, using 1 part of salt to 8 parts ice.

---

4 cups diced rhubarb
1½ cups sugar
2 eggs

2 tablespoons lemon juice
2 cups cream
1 banana, sliced

Rhubarb Ice Cream
European

Clean and dice rhubarb then add sugar and cook at medium heat until rhubarb is soft. Let cool. Beat eggs, add lemon juice, cream and bananas. Stir in rhubarb sauce. Freeze in old-fashioned hand freezer or refrigerator—stirring frequently.

---

2 cups sugar
2 cups boiling water
½ cup crushed mint
Juice of 3 lemons

1 cup cream
3 cups milk
Green coloring if desired

Fresh Mint Ice Cream
Southern

Combine sugar and water and stir until dissolved. Add mint leaves and lemon and let stand 1 hour. Add cream and milk. Beat smooth and freeze in hand freezer.

¼ cup chopped seedless raisins
⅓ cup hot water
1⅓ cups condensed milk
1¼ cups cold water
¼ teaspoon salt

3 egg yolks beaten
2 teaspoons vanilla
¼ cup chopped maraschino
  cherries
2 cups heavy cream

Egg Nog Ice Cream
Southern

Cook raisins in hot water for 5 minutes. Mix condensed milk, water with rest of ingredients and blend well. Add raisins and let cool. Fold in whipped cream and freeze.

---

1 pint milk
1 cup sugar
Grated rind of 2 lemons
Juice of 2 lemons

2 egg whites
2 tablespoons sugar
1 cup cream

Lemon Cream Sherbet
Southern

Add sugar to milk and allow to dissolve. When thoroughly dissolved add lemon rind and juice. Stir while adding lemon juice. Add cream. Beat egg whites with sugar until fluffy and fold into rest of ingredients. Freeze in old-fashioned freezer. Makes 1½ quarts.

⅔ cup sugar
2 cups milk
2 cups cream

¼ teaspoon salt
1 tablespoon vanilla

Old Fashioned Vanilla Ice Cream
Southern

Dissolve thoroughly sugar in milk and cream, add salt and vanilla. Fill freezer ⅔ full and freeze using 3 parts ice to 1 part salt. For fresh fruit ice cream, such as peach, banana, etc., substitute 1 cup fruit pulp for 1 cup milk. For chocolate ice cream substitute 1 cup chocolate syrup for 1 cup milk. Makes 1½ quarts.

Coffee Ice Cream
International

1½ cups cold coffee
24 teaspoons or ½ cup condensed milk (sweetened)
1 cup cream, whipped

Beat coffee and condensed milk together. Fold whipped cream into coffee mixture. Freeze in automatic refrigerator for 2 to 4 hours or until firm. Top with coffee sauce.

Coffee Sauce
International

COFFEE SAUCE FOR ICE CREAM:
½ cup very strong coffee
1 cup sugar
½ cup of evaporated milk
¼ teaspoon salt

Cook coffee and sugar together until mixture forms a soft ball in cold water, or until it reaches 238° on a candy thermometer. Cool to lukewarm. Then stir in evaporated milk and salt.

Mexican Fiesta Ice Cream
Mexico

1 cup mashed peaches
1 cup milk
½ cup sugar
1 tablespoon flour
Dash of salt
2 eggs
1 tablespoon vanilla
1 cup marshmallows (quartered)
½ cup chopped roasted almonds
½ cup chopped green and red Maraschino cherries

Scald milk and add blended mixture of ¼ cup sugar, flour and salt. Cook over low heat until mixture coats a spoon. Add eggs beaten with remaining ¼ cup sugar. Cook 2 minutes longer. Cool and add remaining ingredients. Freeze, using 3 parts ice to 1 part salt. Makes approximately 1 quart.

Parfait
France

1 cup sugar
2 egg whites
Vanilla
¼ cup water
2 cups cream

Boil sugar and water without stirring until it spins a thread. Beat egg whites with a pinch of salt until stiff. Pour the syrup slowly over egg whites, beating continually. When thick, allow to cool. Beat the cream and fold into egg mixture. Season with vanilla. Freeze in ice trays. Serve with crushed fresh fruit.

Biscuit Tortoni
Italy

1 cup heavy cream
¼ cup powdered sugar
⅛ teaspoon salt
1 egg white stiffly beaten
½ teaspoon almond extract or vanilla
1 cup crumbled macaroons

Whip cream with sugar and salt. Fold in stiffly beaten egg white, flavoring and macaroon crumbs. Freeze in paper baking cups for 3 hours. Decorate with cherries and almonds.

Pumpkin Ice Cream
Southern

4 egg yolks
½ cup sugar
4 stiffly beaten egg whites
2 cups heavy cream
1⅓ cups milk
2 cups canned pumpkin
½ cup brown sugar
½ teaspoon salt
½ teaspoon cinnamon
½ teaspoon nutmeg
½ teaspoon allspice
½ teaspoon vanilla

Beat egg yolks. Add sugar, pumpkin, brown sugar, cream, milk and flavorings. Fold in egg whites. Fill freezer ⅔ full and freeze, using 3 parts ice to 1 part salt. Makes approximately ½ gallon when frozen.

1 tablespoon cornstarch
1 cup sugar
¼ cup salt
⅜ cup water
¼ stick butter

3 eggs separated
⅓ cup lemon juice
1 teaspoon grated lemon rind
4 tablespoons rum or
1 teaspoon rum flavoring

Rum Butter Sauce
Southern

Combine cornstarch, sugar, salt and water and cook for 5 minutes, then add butter, beaten egg yolks and lemon juice and rind. Whip egg whites stiff. Fold into cooled sauce. Fold in rum flavoring.

---

4 squares unsweetened chocolate
¾ cup water
1 cup sugar

⅛ teaspoon salt
6 tablespoons butter
½ teaspoon vanilla

Chocolate Sauce Deluxe
Southern

Add chocolate to water and place over low heat. Stir until blended. Add sugar and salt. Cook until sugar has dissolved and mixture is slightly thickened. Add butter and vanilla. Cool. Whipped cream or melted marshmallow may be folded in when sauce is cool.

---

1 cup pressed figs
1 cup pitted dates
1 cup seeded raisins
1 cup candied orange peel

½ cup nuts
2 tablespoons lemon juice
Powdered sugar

Sugar Plums
English

Grind fruits, nuts and add lemon juice. Shape mixture into small balls the size of a plum. Roll in powdered sugar.

---

3 cups vanilla wafers, crushed fine
1 cup finely ground walnuts or pecans

1½ tablespoons cocoa
3 tablespoons dark or light Karo syrup
6 tablespoons bourbon or rum

Whiskey Balls
Southern

Mix all ingredients well and roll into small balls. Dip each ball in powdered sugar. Nice for afternoon tea or with chilled pears.

---

1 cup brown sugar
½ cup oil
¼ cup sour milk
½ teaspoon vanilla
1 cup sifted flour

½ teaspoon salt
½ teaspoon soda
1 teaspoon cinnamon
2 cups 3 minute oats

Oatmeal Cookies
Southern

Beat all ingredients together except oats. After you have a smooth batter, stir in oats. Shape into rounds and bake in a 375° oven for 10 minutes.

1/2 cup shortening
1/2 cup sugar
1 egg

3/4 cup flour
1/4 teaspoon salt
1/2 teaspoon vanilla

Brown Edge Wafers
Southern

Cream shortening and sugar; add rest of ingredients and beat until smooth. Place by teaspoonfuls on lightly greased cooking sheet. Bake in oven of 375 degrees. Remove from sheet immediately, before cooling. These cookies will spread; bake with a brown edge. These are wonderful!

Almond Macaroons
French

½ pound almond paste
3 egg whites
½ cup sifted flour

½ cup fine granulated sugar
½ cup powdered sugar

Work almond paste until smooth. Add the egg whites slightly beaten, and blend thoroughly. Add dry ingredients which have been sifted together. Cover a cookie sheet with plain white paper. Drop from tip of spoon the macaroon mixture. Bake in a 300° oven for 30 minutes. Remove the macaroons from paper while still warm. Store for several days in tin box to mellow.

Swedish Butter Pecan Balls
Sweden

¼ cup butter
3 tablespoons powdered sugar
1 teaspoon vanilla

1 cup flour
1 cup pecans, broken
Pinch salt

Cream butter and sugar until soft and add vanilla, flour, pecans and salt. Work until soft with hands. Mixture is crumbly. Press into small balls and bake in a 300° oven until lightly browned. Roll in powdered sugar while hot. Serve when cold.

Pralines
French

1 pound brown sugar
2 cups pecans

1 tablespoon butter
4 tablespoons water

Cook to soft ball stage in saucepan. Beat until cool. Drop with spoon on waxed paper. Add pecans just before dropping on paper.

Chocolate Fudge
Southern

1 3-ounce package cream cheese
2 cups sifted confectioners sugar
2 1-ounce squares unsweetened chocolate

¼ teaspoon vanilla
Dash of salt
½ cup chopped pecans

Melt chocolate and blend with rest of ingredients except nuts, until smooth. Then add nuts, until smooth. Then add nuts. Place in greased platter. Chill in refrigerator. Cut in squares. This is candy children can make.

Marzipan
German

1 egg white
1 cup almond paste

3 cups confectioners sugar

Beat egg whites until fluffy. Gradually work in almond paste. Add confectioners sugar and knead until it makes a paste that is easy to handle. If paste becomes too stiff add lemon juice drop by drop. If it becomes too moist add more sugar. Form into long rolls. Color and shape into tiny fruits and vegetables, using a seed catalogue to copy from. Attach stems and leaves and let dry 2 to 3 hours before applying glaze.

GLAZE:
½ cup sugar

¾ cup water
½ cup light corn syrup

Combine all ingredients and bring to a good boil. Boil for about 2 minutes or until it reaches 220° F. Apply while hot to candy, using small paint brush. Let dry.

1½ sticks butter
2 cups sugar
2 eggs
6 cups sifted flour
6 teaspoons baking powder
  (scant)

2 teaspoons nutmeg
1 tablespoon vanilla
1 tablespoon rosewater
Approx. 1⅓ cups milk (enough
  to form soft dough)

Old Fashion Tea Cakes
Southern

Cream butter and sugar. Add eggs and beat thoroughly. Mix and sift dry ingredients. Add to creamed mixture alternately with milk. Add flavoring. Let stand for 4 hours to ripen. Roll out in 4 inch rounds and bake in a 325° oven until light brown. Sprinkle with sugar.

---

1 1/4 sticks butter
1 1/2 cups flour
Powdered sugar

1/4 cup sugar
Jelly
Pecan halves, if desired

Thumb Print Cookies
Southern

Cream butter, sugar and flour. Shape into balls about the size of a marble. Take thumb and press into ball and flatten out. Put a small dab of jelly (tart) in thumb print. Bake in 300 degree oven untill browned lightly. While hot, place a pecan half on jelly and sprinkle with powdered sugar.

A little almond flavoring and a dab of almond paste, instead of jelly, is a company treat.

---

1 small potato
1 pound confectioners sugar

½ teaspoon flavoring
2 drops food coloring

Mashed Potato Patty Mints
Southern

Boil potato with peeling on until tender. Peel potato, beat until fluffy. While still hot gradually add confectionery sugar until desired stiffness to mold. Add flavoring and food coloring. Use decorating tube to shape. Let dry 24 hours.

---

1 stick butter
1 lb powdered sugar
1 large semi-sweet candy bar
1 - 2 Tbs. paraffin

2 cups crunchy peanut butter
3 cups rice crispies
1 6 oz package chocolate chips

Peanut Butter Balls
Southern

Mix first three ingredients until smooth. Add rice crispies. Shape into balls and chill. Then dip into melted chocolate chips, candy bar and paraffin (combine & melt the last three ingredients in top of double boiler) use a fork to dip balls into chocolate. Coat well and allow to set up.

---

3 cups sugar
1 cup honey
1 1/4 cups shortening
1/2 cup cut almonds
3 eggs
1 tsp cinnamon
1 tsp soda   Enough flour to make a stiff dough (approx. 7 cups)

1 cup molasses
2 Tbs brandy
1 1/2 cups chopped nuts
1/2 cup chopped citron
1 tsp salt
1 tsp cloves

Lebkuchen (Delicious German Cakes)
German

Put molasses honey and sugar into a kettle and boil 5 minutes. While hot add shortening, 4 cups of flour, spices and nuts. when nearly cold, add soda dissolved in 1 cup boiling water. Add well-beaten eggs and flour to make a stiff dough. Let stand 3 or 4 days. Roll out. Bake in 350° oven. Frost with water and powdered sugar glaze (1 Tbs hot water, 1 cup powdered sugar). Decorate with almonds.

Sandbakkels
Scandinavian

1 cup crisco	1 cup butter
1 1/2 cups brown sugar	2 eggs
5 cups flour	1 tsp ground cardamon

Cream crisco, butter and sugar. Add eggs and flour. Chill dough and press into baking tins. Bake in 350⁰ oven about 10 minutes until lightly brown. Allow to cool for a few minutes then tap out of tins.

Cathedral Windows
Southern

4 Tbs. butter	1 12 oz. Pkg. semisweet
2 eggs, well beaten	chocolate chips
1 10 1/2 oz. pkg. colored miniature	1 cup chopped pecans
marshmallows	powdered sugar

Melt butter and chocolate in top of double boiler. Cool - beat in eggs. Fold in marshmallows and pecans (if desired). Pour into a 9 X 5 loaf pan lined with foil. Chill until firm. Remove from pan and slice very thin

Lollipops
International

2 cups sugar	½ teaspoon cinnamon extract
1 cup water	½ teaspoon red food coloring
1½ teaspoons anise extract or	

Cook sugar, corn syrup and water to a hard ball stage (295° to 300°). Remove from heat and when bubbling stops add extract and food coloring. Drop by the tablespoonful onto wooden skewers on an oiled cooky sheet. Makes 30.

Caramel Candy
Southern

2/3 cup sugar	1/4 cup margarine or butter

Brown or melt 2/3 cup of sugar in an iron skillet. Add 1/4 cup of margarine or butter. Mix.

2 1/3 cups of sugar	1 cup milk
1 cup cream	1/2 cup light Karo syrup

Put these ingredients in a large sauce pan. Bring the milk mixture to a rolling boil. Add melted sugar to the mixture. Cook over medium heat until a teaspoon of the mixture is found firm when dropped into a cup of cool water.

Remove from heat and cool the mixture somewhat by beating it with a large spoon.

Pour into a buttered dish. Cool. Cut into 1 inch squares.

Peanut Brittle
Southern

2 cups white sugar	1 scant cup white syrup
1 cup water	(I use Bob White)

Cook to soft ball stage.
Add: 1 teaspoon oleo and 2 heaping cups unroasted peanuts. Cook to hard ball or till peanuts are roasted. Take off of heat. Add 2 teaspoons baking soda and 1 teaspoon vanilla. Stir just enough to mix and pour in greased pan as soon as possible. Cool till easily removed from pans (not cool) and break into pieces. If you let it get cold, its liable to get sticky. Keep in air tight containers.

1 qt. molasses
    (Grandmas - Ber Rabbit)
2 T soda (dissolved in small
    amount water & added to
    above mixture)
2 T cinnamon

(I double the above and add
nutmeg and allspice)

12 oz. brown sugar
12 oz shortening
2 T ginger
2 T cloves
1/4 t salt
3 1/2 lb flour - sift with spices to
mix
well

Molasses or Moravian Thin Cookies
Czechoslovakia

This should be a stiff dough. Let stand over night to roll better. Roll on a well floured board*. Roll very thin. Lift with spatula to place on pans. Bake at 325⁰ for 5 minutes.

---

3 eggs, room temperature
1 cup plus 2 tablespoons sugar
1 3/4 cups sifted flour
1/2 teaspoon baking powder

1/2 teaspoon salt
3 teaspoons anise seed or 1
    teaspoon anise extract

Anisplattz-Chen
Germany

Beat eggs in mixer until fluffy and add the sugar gradually beating continously. Continue to beat for 20 minutes. Add the dry ingredients which have been sifted together and beat for another three minutes. Add anise. Drop on well greased and floured cookie sheets and from a round cookie by swirling the dough with a spoon. Let stand to dry over night. Bake at 325 degrees for about 15 minutes or until cookies are a light golden color. Yield about 3 1/2 dozen cookies.
(Don't even try these unless you like anise)

---

2 cups sugar
1 cup butter
2 cups flour

2/3 cup cocoa
4 eggs
1 teaspoon vanilla

Marshmallow Brownies with Frosting

Cream sugar and butter, add rest of ingredients. Press into greased 9 x 14 inch baking pan. Bake 25 minutes at 300 degrees. Then spread with 1 package colored minature marshmallows. Bake 5 minutes longer. Cool cake for 1 hour then frost.

1/3 cup canned milk
1 stick butter
6 ounces chocolate chips (semi-sweet)

1 cup sugar
1 teaspoon vanilla

Chocolate Butter Frosting

Mix all ingredients, bring to boil. Boil 1 minute. Beat slightly and pour over marshmallow brownies. Cool before cutting.

BEVERAGES

THAT intangible and mysterious thing called Opportunity about which so many essays have been written, so many sermons preached and so many poems inspired is not a stranger who comes and knocks at our door in disguise—not a winged meteor that spreads its flaring stream of light across the heavens when least expected and not an archangel that suddenly awakens us from our sleep to bring good tidings.

Opportunity is just plain home folk.

It's as constant as the shadows that walk with us, and is always present in our affairs—regardless of vocation, position or circumstances.

Opportunity is not what may come to us to-morrow but what we make out of to-day.

For each cup:
1 heaping teaspoon pulverized coffee

1 heaping teaspoon sugar
1 small cup water

Turkish Coffee
Turkey

Put all ingredients in a small pot. Bring to a boil and remove from heat. Shake. Bring back to boil. Shake 3 times or whip. Pour into cups. The grounds will settle in each cup. Flavor coffee if desired with orange blossom water or cardamon seed.

---

2 tablespoons lemon crystals
6 tablespoons strained honey

2 cups hot boiling water
1 cup brandy

Hot Honey Punch
Africa

Add lemon crystals and honey to boiling water. Stir until blended. Add 1 cup brandy and serve in punch cups with a sprinkling of ground nutmeg.

Pronouncing Your Wine Names

Aligoté	*ah-lee-go-tay*
Aloxe-Corton	*ah-loss cor-tawn*
Alsace	*al-sass*
Apéritif	*ah-pair-ee-teef*
Beaune	*bone*
Blanc-de-Blancs	*blawn-duh-blawn*
Bodega	*bo-day-ga*
Bourgeois	*boor-zwah*
Chambertin	*shawm-bair-tan*
Corbières	*cor-be-air*
Côte de Nuits	*coat-duh-nwee*
Cuvée	*coo-vay*
Fixin	*feex-an*
Frizzante	*freez-zahn-tay*
Gattinara	*got-tee-nah-ra*
Grand Vin	*grawn-van*
Grignolino	*green-yo-lee-no*
Haut-Médoc	*oh-may-dawk*
Hermitage	*air-mee-taj*
Jerez	*hair-eth*
Lambrusco	*lom-bruce-co*
Loire	*lwahr*
Macon	*mac-cawn*
Meursault	*mere-so*
Nebbiolo	*neb-bee-oh-lo*
Orvieto	*or-vee-ate-toe*
Petit Syrah	*puh-tee see-rah*
Pinot Chardonnay	*pee-no shar-doe-nay*
Pommard	*po-mar*
Puligny-Montrachet	*poo-leen-yee mawn-rash-shay*
Riquevihr	*reek-veer*
Ruwer	*roo-ver*
Saint-Emilion	*sant a-mee-lee-awn*
Sancerre	*sawn-sair*
Sangria	*sahn-gree-ah*
Sauvignon	*so-veen-yawn*
Secco	*say-ko*
Sommelier	*so-mel-yay*
Spumante	*spoo-mahn-tay*
Tastevin	*tat-van*
Valpolicella	*vahl-po-lee-chella*
Velouté	*vel-loo-tay*
Vendange	*vawn-dawnj*
Verdicchio	*vair-dee-key-o*
Vigneron	*veen-yair-rawn*
Vin Blanc	*van blawn*
Vosne-Romanée	*vone-ro-ma-nay*

Boiled Coffee
Southern

Allow 1 heaping Tbs of coffee for each cup. Fill a clean pot with water allowing room to boil up. Add coffee to water and allow to boil up. Remove from heat, let cool 5 minutes. Place back on heat and allow to boil up again. Remove from heat. Let stand a few minutes for coffee grounds to settle. Serve.

Its delicious.

Chocolate
(instant hot chocolate)
Southern

1 box instant milk
8 tablespoons unsweetened cocoa
1 pound box of instant chocolate drink

1 16 ounce size instant cream
1 pound powdered sugar

Mix all together and keep in closed crock or jar. Use two or three teaspoons to a cup of boiling water. An excellent Christmas gift tied with a gay bow. (Makes eight quarts of mix.)

Instant Spiced Tea
Southern

2 cups sugar
1 pound jar orange breakfast drink
1 teaspoon ground cinnamon

1 cup instant plain tea
1 teaspoon ground cloves
1 large package of instant lemonade mix

Mix above ingredients and place in airtight container. To serve, put two teaspoons in cup of hot water for hot tea. This same mix also makes excellent iced tea.

Egg Nog
Southern

12 eggs, separated
1/2 pint Jamaica rum
1 pint bourbon

1 qt. double cream, whipped
12 rounded tablespoons sugar

Beat egg yolks until very light and fluffy. Gradually stir in sugar. Add whiskey and rum slowly while beating. Fold in whipped cream and stiffly beaten egg whites just before serving. (Makes 24 servings.)

Home-Made Wine
Southern

20 pounds berries or grapes
10 cups sugar

5 quarts boiling water

Mash:
20 pounds berries or grapes in large stone crock. Add 5 quarts boiling water. Cover and let stand 3 days.

Strain contents through cheescloth. Return juice to the crock and add 10 cups sugar.

Place crock in pan to catch juices that overflow while wine is working. Cover crock and let stand until fermentation has cleared. Remove scum.

Strain and bottle with a tight seal.

2 cups sugar
2 cups water
10 cloves
1 2-inch stick cinnamon
½ teaspoon ginger

½ cup lemon juice
2 cups orange juice
2 drops oil of peppermint
Mint leaves
Green coloring if desired

Boil sugar and water for 5 minutes. Add spices and let stand until cool. Add fruit juices. Strain. Color pale green, and add peppermint. Let stand for 2 hours. Pour over crushed ice and garnish with mint leaves.

---

1 quart milk
1 inch stick cinnamon
3 tablespoons strong coffee
2 squares sweet chocolate

½ cup boiling water
1 tablespoon vanilla
⅛ teaspoon salt
½ teaspoon nutmeg

Heat milk with cinnamon and coffee. Melt chocolate in ½ cup boiling water and add to milk mixture. Add vanilla, salt and nutmeg. Heat to scalding. Beat slightly and serve frothy hot.

---

2 eggs, well beaten
8 teaspoons instant coffee
10 teaspoons sugar

4 cups chilled milk
½ teaspoon vanilla

Beat eggs. Add coffee and sugar. Beat until sugar is dissolved and mixture is smooth. Add milk and vanilla. Serve in punch cups.

1½ cups boiling water
3 teaspoons tea
¾ cup confectioners sugar
½ cup lemon juice

Grated rind of 3 lemons
2 cups grape juice
2¼ cups pineapple juice
1 quart gingerale

Pour water over tea. Let steep for 3 minutes, then strain. Dissolve sugar in lemon juice and add to tea. Mix with all other ingredients. Chill with crushed ice. Delicious party punch.

---

1 quart tea
½ teaspoon clove and a few whole cloves

½ teaspoon allspice
½ teaspoon cinnamon or 1 stick
2 tablespoons blackberry jam

Simmer all ingredients. Serve hot.

---

1 gallon cider
1 lemon peel

2 sticks cinnamon
¼ cup honey

Simmer ingredients together for 30 minutes. Serve piping hot.

---

1 pint cranberry juice cocktail
1 bottle gingerale

1 pint lemon sherbert
Lemon peel

Combine cranberry juice cocktail and gingerale. Add sherbert by spoonfuls and garnish with twisted lemon peel.

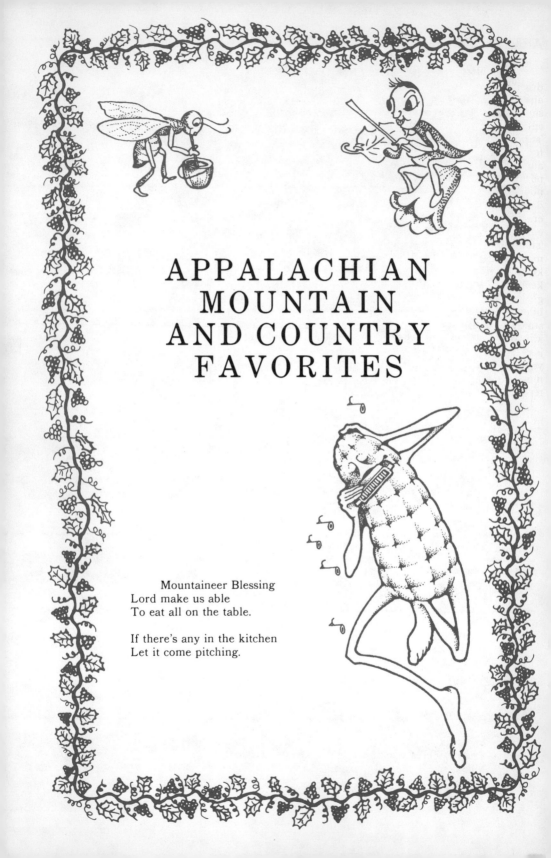

APPALACHIAN MOUNTAIN AND COUNTRY FAVORITES

Mountaineer Blessing
Lord make us able
To eat all on the table.

If there's any in the kitchen
Let it come pitching.

GLOSSARY OF COUNTRY DIALECT

dreen	-	drain	tase	-	taste
air	-	are	vittles	-	food
sho	-	sure	fraish	-	fresh
agin	-	again	lif	-	lift
'stidder	-	in stead of	fo'	-	four
fer	-	for	aigs	-	eggs
aint	-	isn't	kilt	-	killed
po'	-	poor	drap	-	-drop
houn'	-	hound	okry	-	okra
dawg	-	dog	'taters	-	potatoes
er	-	of	cawn	-	corn
em	-	them	sarvin	-	serving
'stonishin	-	astonishing	fergit	-	forget
mawnin	-	morning	tother	-	the other
kiver	-	cover	sich	-	such
keerful	-	careful	whupped	-	whipped
git	-	get	holpin'	-	helping
bile	-	boil	younguns	-	little ones
stiddy	-	steady	som'ers	-	somewhere
kin	-	can	poke	-	sack
jes	-	just			
yo'	-	your			
mus'	-	must			
ter	-	to			

Take time to understand us.
You will like it!

Expressions You Might Hear in the Mountains

I dogged if I know	I don't know
Aw shucks	Really
He come back	He came back
They git sheda	Get rid of
Chock full	Filled up
Stone col'	Ice cold
Pretty nigh	Almost
If you've a min	If you like
Yer innards	Your stomach
Lef ter yer gumption	Left to your judgment
Go fetch it	Go get it
Too yer whistle	Talk too much
This here's fittin	Really good
Mess or batch	Good amount
Tote the grub	Carry the food
Moonshining	Making corn liquor
Rite smart	Quite a bit

Dig a pit the size that is required for the amount of meat you have. A small hole is about 9 inches deep - say for a grill space up to 2 feet square. For large barbecues, I like a pit dug about 12 to 18 inches deep, 3 to 4 feet wide and as long as you wish. Never get your pit so wide that you can't safely tend your fire and barbecue.

Never start to barbecue until your fire and coals have died down. keep a fire of hickory wood going to continue feeding coals to the pit. This fire should be close to the pit. We call this the feeder fire.

Open Pit Barbecue
Southern

We use heavy chicken wire frames to stretch across our pits. These should be a few inches above the embers. New brooms or mops are used to brush large portions of meat with the sop. Warm salted water is used to baste the meat until it gets hot enough to keep away insects and flies.

We then use the same sop or mopping sauce as for oven barbecue. Allow 12 to 18 hours to cook large pieces of meat over open pit.

For a good mopping sauce recipe for larger amounts of meat (20 to 30 pounds) use:

1 quart apple cider vinegar
1 stick butter
3 tablespoons crushed hot red
pepper
Salt and pepper to taste
1 lemon, sliced thin
Bring to a boil and sop.

They's stews an' stews, honey, but ter my min' th' ain't nothin' so satisfyin' as ol' time brunswick stew. some folks holts that brunswick stew air gotta be made outer squir'l but they's others what thinks nothin' cyarn't beat chicken. Since we got a chicken kilt an' picked an' cut up ready an' the squir'ls air still a hoppin' from limb ter limb in the park I reckon we'll take chicken this time an' save the squir'l rule till campin' out time.

Salt an' pepper yo' j'inted chicken an' roll it in flour. Now cut up a half poun'er salt po'k inter a hot skillet an' drap yo' chicken in an' brown it slow an' keerful long with po'k. Slice up two good sized onions an' fry 'em in the skillet with chicken an' chicken fixin's.

Now scrape out all the contempts er the skillet inter yo' big 'lulimum pot. Kiver it with 'bout a quart er water. Open up a big can er termattersies an' dump it in. If you air so sitchumated you kin git fraish vegtables so much the better but brunswick stew made outer canned things ain't ter say nasty. Now a can er butterbeans, one er okry an' three good sized Irish 'taters peeled an' cut up fineish.

Brunswick Stew
Southern

Ain't it got no cawn in it? Yes, honey, but too much cookin' makes cawn hard an' I never puts it in the pot till 'bout five minutes befo' sarvin'. Now throw in a han'ful er rice an' season keerful. That's where the gumption comes in. When the stew comes ter a good bubblin' bile turn yo' fire down real low an' go off an' fergit it.

Brunswick stew oughter be good an' thickish. When the time comes ter sarve it an' you done added the can er cawn, or the fraish cawn as the case may be, if it air too juicy like, you kin thicken the mess either with flour or with a iron spoon er cooked oatmeal. I favors col' oatmeal as a thickenin'. It air smooth an' somehow don't tas'e so starchy. On the days you have this here stew 'tain't wuth while ter cook up no mo' victuals. It air a meal in itself.

Fried: Select center cut slices from an 18 month old ham (a 2 year ham is even better). Slice ham about 1/4 inch thick. Trim off skin. Place slices in ungreased <u>hot</u> skillet and fry quickly on both sides. Remove ham to hot platter and make red-eye gravy out of drippings by adding 4 tablespoons black coffee to skillet. Let it sizzle up and pour over ham.
Serve with grits!

Boiled: (In oven)
Soak whole ham overnight in cold water. (Cut off hock end.)
Place in deep pan and almost cover ham with warm water. Place in oven and cook in 300 degree temperature, allowing 20 minutes to the pound.

An 18 pound ham will take 6 hours.

Remove skin while hot. Make a mixture using 1/2 cup cornmeal and 1/2 cup brown sugar. Pat over top of skinned ham. Run back into 450 degree oven and brown.

Chill thoroughly before slicing.

Country hams should be sliced very thin.

Country Ham
Southern

When I asked Granny Nanny about these, her eyes lit up!
"Sho' I kin cook 'em. Chitlins is men folks food. Women folks holt theyselves above chitlins.

You kin buy chitlins from yo butcher all cleaned an' ready ter cook.
First you put them on ter parbile in salt an' water with a red pepper an' a han' full of cloves.
* *I mus 'fes up, chitlins don't smell like jewraniums whilst they air bilin- jes shut yo' ketchen off from the house an' open the back do' for a spell.*
When they air tender, take em out an let em dreen. Then cut em up in pieces 'bout as big as selected oysters. Now roll em in flour or else beaten aig an' cracker crumbs. Fry in deep fat. Maughty tasty! Salt and pepper em good!"

Chitterlings (Chittlins)
Southern

(This makes your tongue wag!)

1 pound tripe	Boiling water
1 pound liver	1 skunk egg (onion)
1 pound heart	Salt and pepper to taste
1 pound brains	1 pod red pepper
1/4 pound suet	

Cut up all ingredients. Cover with boiling water. Season with salt, pepper, onion and red pepper. Simmer over low heat 3 to 4 hours. Thicken with 2 tablespoons flour blended with cold water. This is so good!

Mother-in-Law Stew
Appalachian

An extremely delicious dish if you do it right!

First, catch your possum alive during the late fall after he has fattened up on persimmons. Kill as you would a piglet - scald and clean by splitting down through the stomach.

Soak in milk overnight.

Roast Opossum or Groundhog
Appalachian

Rinse well and sprinkle cavity with poultry seasoning, a crushed bay leaf and a dash or two of allspice.

Place in pan with 2 cups boiling water.
Cover with butter and sear for 20 minutes in a very hot oven.

Reduce heat to 300 degrees and cover pan.
Bake for 3 to 4 hours until tender. Remove lid, brush with heavy cream and bake until brown.
Serve on a large platter.

Surround with sweet potatoes (baked in their skins or you may peel the sweet potatoes and bake the last hour with the possum).

Prepare groundhog or any wild game in the same manner.
Wild turkey and geese are delightful prepared this way too.

Mountain Oysters (Calf Fries)
Appalachian

Testicles cut form bull calves when they are made into steers.

Clean the oysters, soak in ice water - dredge with flour and fry in hot fat until well browned. Sprinkle with salt an pepper and serve with scrambled eggs and buttermilk biscuits.

Turtle and Frog Legs (Fried)
Appalachian

Prepare frog legs and turtle. Soak overnight in refrigerator in buttermilk. Allow to stand 2 hours at room temperature. Then dip in flour and fry as you would chicken.
I have found that heating the buttermilk slightly greatly improves the flavor of the turtle meat and frog legs.

Fresh Backbone and Sauerkraut or Turnips
Appalachian

Simmer backbone with water to cover, salt and pepper to taste, until tender - 4 or 5 hours. Cook turnips or sauerkraut in the broth and serve hot.
'Tis worth moving to the country to taste this!

Lye Hominy
Appalachian

1 gallon Hickory cane shelled dry corn	8 pounds lye 4 gallons water

Use iron kettle. Dissolve lye in water, add corn. Bring to a boil and boil 30 minutes or until hulls loosen. Rinse corn through several hot water rinses to remove lye. Cover with cold water and rub corn to remove hulls and black tips. Let stand in fresh water 3 hours. (Changing water 4 times.) Drain, cover with boiling salted water, 1 teaspoon salt to each quart water. Boil until tender.

1 fat hog's head,
8 pigs feet (4 if you like)
1 cup vinegar

2 tablespoons salt
2 red pepper pods
Enough water to cover

Place all ingredients in a big enamel pot and simmer for 24 hours.
Pick the meat from bones and remove all the gristle. Place in bowl (it will be a mushy mass). Mix with the following seasonings:

1 tablespoon crushed mixed
spices (pickling)
1/4 teaspoon red pepper
1 tablespoon cracked pepper
1 bay leaf, crushed
2 cloves chopped garlic

While hot put into a cheese cloth bag and shape into a flat cake 2 inches thick. Tie bag and press with weight and allow to chill. Slice and serve.

Head Cheese (Souse) (Hogshead Cheese)
Appalachian

---

3 pounds pork liver & lights   Salt and pepper to tast

Cut up liver and lights in 1 inch pieces. Wash thoroughly. Pour scalding water over them and parboil for 30 minutes. Drain off this water and put fresh water in pot - add salt and pepper and sage to taste. Simmer for 4 to 5 hours over low heat.

Hog killing time in the country is a memorable occasion. Neighbors pitch in and help one another. They then share the liver, lights and fresh backbone in appreciation.

So - unless you help at hog killings, you are not apt to taste this delectable dish.

Liver and Lights Stew (Pluck)
Appalachian

Marinate bear steak overnight in:

2 cups red wine
1 tsp worcestershire sauce
2 whole cloves

2 cups vinegar
1 bay leaf
1/4 tsp salt

Dry meat and cut into cubes. Roll meat in flour and fry in small amount of fat until browned.

Put meat in casserole and pour over following mixture:

1/2 cup water
1/2 tsp crushed bay leaf
1/3 tsp garlic

1/3 tsp salt
1 chopped onion
pepper to taste

Cover and bake at 300° for 3 hours. Add more water if necessary. Thicken gravy if desired.

Bear Steak
Appalachian

---

4 cucumbers
Celery salt, pepper and nutmeg
1½ teaspoons grated onion

1 teaspoon lemon juice
1 tablespoon water
½ cup cracker crumbs

Slice cucumbers ½ inch thick. Place in a greased casserole dish. Sprinkle with rest of ingredients. Top with cracker crumbs and butter. Bake in a 375° oven for 40 minutes covered. Uncover and bake for 15 minutes longer.

Scalloped Cucumber
Appalachian

1 medium tomato for each person   Cornmeal
Bacon drippings   Salt and pepper to taste

Fried Tomatoes
Appalachian

Slice tomatoes 1/4 inch thick and roll in cornmeal. Fry in bacon drippings and sprinkle with salt and pepper.

Here in the country we like our vegetables cooked quickly and served piping hot with gobs of butter.

A little dash of sugar is a flavor perker upper for fresh vegetables. Try it · you'll like it.

---

1 pound sausage   1 can hominy (No. 2½)
1 green pepper, chopped   1 teaspoon sugar
4 stalks celery, chopped   1 can tomatoes (No. 2½)
1 onion   Salt and pepper to taste
2 cloves garlic

Hominy Casserole
Appalachian

Crumble and cook sausage until done but not brown. Add green pepper, celery, onion and garlic. Saute until vegetables are about one-half done. Grind hominy through food chopper. Mix with sausage and vegetables. Add sugar tomatoes and salt and pepper. Turn into casserole dish and bake for 35 to 40 minutes in a 350° oven.

---

2 cups corn meal   ½ cup water
1 teaspoon salt   1 egg, beaten
3 teaspoons baking powder   ½ to 1 cup cracklings
½ cup skimmed milk

Crackling Bread
Appalachian

Heat cracklings in water until they boil. Mix corn meal, salt, baking powder, milk and egg. Blend thoroughly. Add cracklings and water. Shape into pones and bake in a 400° oven until brown.

---

2 cups buttermilk   ¼ teaspoon garlic salt
1 cup meal   1 egg
1 teaspoon salt   ½ stick butter
1 teaspoon soda

Fried Mush Cakes
Appalachian

Scald buttermilk then stir in meal, salt, soda, garlic salt, egg and butter. Mix well. Drop by teaspoonfuls on hot griddle and fry with plenty of fat.

1½ cups corn meal   ½ teaspoon soda
½ cup corn   1 egg beaten
2 tablespoons flour   3 tablespoons chopped onion
½ teaspoon salt   1 cup buttermilk

Hush Puppies
Southern

Mix dry ingredients; add beaten egg, onion and buttermilk. Mix well and drop by teaspoons into hot deep fat. When they float they are done. Makes 20-25.

Poke and Eggs
Southern

Parboil 2 pounds of poke in salt water until tender. Drain. Place in skillet with 6 tablespoons bacon drippings and simmer until all water is cooked out of poke. Scramble 6 eggs with poke. Add salt and pepper to taste.

3 cups cooked bunch beans (hot)
2 tablespoons bacon grease
3 slices crisp chopped bacon
¼ cup vinegar
1 tablespoon sugar
1 medium onion, chopped
Salt and pepper

Green Bean Salad
Southern

Add all ingredients to hot beans. Set aside to cool. Serve on salad plates from bowl.

---

2 cups finely chopped cabbage
2 green peppers, finely chopped
1 teaspoon celery seed
2 tablespoons brown sugar
¼ teaspoon mustard seed
¼ cup vinegar
Salt and pepper to taste

Fresh Relish
Southern

Mix well. Let stand for 2 hours in refrigerator.

---

1 cup vinegar
½ cup molasses
or Sorghum
1/2 teaspoon garlic powder, or juice
1 teaspoon dry mustard
1/2 cup sweet pickle juice
1/4 teaspoon cayenne
1 tablespoon salt
1/2 cup of salad oils
(any one you wish to use)
1 cups tomato juice, any brand
1 teaspoon celery
1/2 teaspoon chili powder
1/2 teaspoon black pepper
1 teaspoon paprika

Dressing or Barbeque Sauce
Southern

Just mix together. It makes a little more than a quart. It keeps well in the refrigerator or unrefrigerated.

Place hog jowl in pot with about 1 quart water and a pod of red pepper. Let boil for 1 hour. Then add 1 gallon of cleaned turnip greens. Sprinkle with salt and pepper and add a pinch of soda. Stir well. Cook covered about 1 hour until tender.

We like whole turnips dropped in the pot and cooked with the greens.

Turnip Greens and Hog Jowl
Southern

Drink the Pot Likker!

It's good for you.

Soak 1 lb. white beans overnight. Cook white beans in a large pan with 7 cups water, 1 ham bone, 1 pod red pepper and 1 big onion. Simmer for about 3 hours over low heat until done. Serve with sliced raw onions and corn pone.

White Beans
Southern

---

2 cups blackeyed peas
¼ pound jowl
1 cup rice, cooked
6 cups water
1 onion, sliced
Salt to taste

Hopping John
Southern

Soak peas overnight. Put in kettle with jowl and water. Simmer until tender. Add onion to mixture. When done add rice and salt. Serve hot.

Stuffed Onions
as told by
"Granny Nanny" Southern

"Count yo' folks an' then take that many Bermudy onions an' three over fer good measure or maybe fer a extry mouth that mought drop in an' maybe a pa'r er laigs under that table what seem like they air hollow. Scoop the middle outer them onions after you air peeled 'em. Now make a stuffing outer braid crumbs and lef over meat you happen ter have handy. Run yo' meat and crumbs through the grinder an' season up high with salt and pepper, a dash er wooste sass an' one er termatter ketchup. Blend in some butter. Stuff the onions tight and mound up high. Put a little water in yo' pan and stan' the onions up close together. Kivva. Bake 30 minutes at 350 degrees. Then take off kivva and brown fer about 20 mo' minutes.

Use yo' gumption 'bout selectin' onions. All 'bout the same bigness an' the mo' bigger they air, the better fer stuffin'."

Fire Place Cookery
Southern

Wrap corn with shucks still on in aluminum foil. Dip first in warm water before wrapping in foil. Throw into the hot coals and let steam for 30 minutes. The shucks keep the corn from scorching.

Potatoes can be wrapped in foil, covered with clay pack and cooked in coals.

All meats are excellent this way. For each 2 pounds of meat, allow 1 hour of cooking in clay pack.

When the electricity fails and we have to return to pioneer methods of cooking over the open fire, we love it. We get out our old iron skillets, Dutch ovens and go to work. A big iron soup pot hangs from the pot crane and simmers away. We add this and that to the pot to make a real country soup.

We make stick burgers - hamburgers shaped around the end of a long stick. This is turned over the fire until done, then slipped off the stick and plopped on buns with gobs of onions and mustard.

Drying Vegetables
Southern

Slice vegetables. Steam them in colander over boiling hot water until hot through.

Spread out on pans 1/2 inch deep. Dry in 140° oven 6 to 24 hours, until bone dry.

To reconstitute, soak 1 - 3 hours using 6-8 times amount of water. Use vegtables and water in soups and stews.

Drying Fruits for Winter
Southern

apples, pears, peaches	6 Tbs salt
1 cup sugar	1 gallon cold water

Peel fruit and cut in 1/4 inch slices. Combine salt, sugar and water, stir until salt and sugar have dissolved. Place sliced fruit in solution for several minutes. Spread out on platter or racks and dry in sun for 3 days (taking in at night). Make oven-dried in 140° oven for 6 to 24 hours. Dry until leathery. Store in cool place in air tight container to keep insects out.

They ain't nothin' what makes a pleasanter change than sweet 'tater biscuit. No, honey, they ain't so hard ter make if you puts in one part er gumption ter ev'y part er other ingrediums. Take two cups er flour an' three teaspoons er bakin' powder an' a sacnt spoon er salt an' sif' it all through inter a bowl. Rub inter er yo' flour a hunk er lard 'bout the size of a mejum aig an' a cup er sweet 'taters what air been biled an' mashed an' beat up light with a tablespoon er butter an' one er sugar an' a half cup er cream. Now add enough sweet milk ter make a sof' dough an' roll it out thinnish 'cordin' ter what part er the country yo' folks come from. Folks down Souf likes they biscuits thin an' folks up Norf likes 'em fat. The makin's air the same an' the bakin' air the same. Have yo' oven hot an' fer Gawd's sake don't cook yo' biscuit ahead er time, but bring 'em in pipin' hot, so's they pretty nigh burn the folks's fingers when they holp theyselves.

Sweet Potato Biscuits
Southern

---

2 cups plain flour
1/2 teaspoon salt
1/2 cup crisco
1/2 cup sweet milk

1 teaspoon soda
1 package onion soup mix (dry)
1/4 cup apple cider vinegar
Caraway seeds and coarse salt

Salty Dogs
Appalachian

Combine flour, soda, salt and dry onion soup mix. Work in 1/2 cup crisco with fingers. Add vinegar to sweet milk and combine all at once with dry ingredients. Shape dough into small fingers and roll lightly in salt and caraway seeds. Bake in slow 275 degree oven until brown and crisp.

---

5 lb brown sugar
1 1/4 tsp salt
3/4 lb oleo (melted)
2 T vanilla

8 lb whole wheat flour
2 T soda
1 1/2 tsp maple flavor
2 1/2 qt. buttermilk or sour milk

Homemade Grape Nuts
Southern

Put dry ingredients in bowl except soda which should be added to milk just before adding milk to dry ingredients. Last add oleo and flavorings. Mix well. Dough should be fairly thick. If too thick, add milk. If too thin, add flour. Put in pans and spread even. Bake in 350° oven till baked. Take out and let cool. Rub over wire netting, or over a grater. Dry in oven till crisp. Makes 15 lb grape-nuts.

---

1 stick butter
¼ cup brown sugar
1 cup flour

Shortening Bread
Southern

Cream butter, sugar and flour. Add flavoring
Press out to ½ inch thickness on floured board. Cut in squares and bake in 325° oven until brown.

½ pint white corn meal
½ teaspoon salt

2 tablespoons melted shortening
Cold water

Corn Meal Dodgers
Southern

Mix ingredients and add just enough cold water to make a very stiff dough. Shape into small round biscuits. Drop in hot boiling pot likker and cover. Cook 20 minutes.

4 cups flour	1 tablespoon cornstarch
1 teacup full of lard	1 teaspoon salt
1 tablespoon sugar	1 cup ice water

Beaten Biscuits
Southern

Combine flour, sugar, cornstarch and salt. Using fingertips work in lard until mixture is very fine. Add the ice water to make a stiff dough. Beat the dough flat, fold and beat for 400 strokes or use a beaten biscuit roller and roll and beat until the dough looks like baby skin. Roll out, cut into little biscuits. Prick with fork and bake 1 hour at 300 degrees until dried out. DO NOT brown. Makes 72.

Salt Rising Bread
Southern

On the night before take ½ cup of corn meal and a pinch of salt and sugar. Scald this with milk heated to the boiling point and mix to the thickness of mush. This can be made in a cup. Wrap in a clean cloth and put in a warm place overnight.

In the morning, when all is ready, take a one-gallon stone jar and into this put one scant cup of milk. Add a level teaspoon of salt and 1 of sugar. Scald this with three cups of water heated to the boiling point. Reduce to a temperature of 180° with cold water, using a milk thermometer to enable you to get exactly the right temperature. Then add flour and mix to a good batter; after the batter is made, mix in your starter that was made the night before. Cover the stone jar with a plate and put the jar in a large kettle of water and keep this water at a temperature of 108° until the sponge rises. It should rise at least an inch and a half. When it has raised mix to a stiff dough, make into loaves and put into pans. Do not let the heat get out of the dough while working. Grease the loaves well on top and set your board where it will be warm and rise. After the loaves rise bake in a medium oven for 1 hour and 10 minutes. When you take the loaves from the oven wrap them in a breadcloth.

---

2 cups meal	1 teaspoon salt
1 cup cold water	Handful of flour
2 cups boiling water	

Corn Light Bread
Southern

Combine cold water with meal. Stir in boiling water. Cook until a thick mush. Cool with about 1 cup cold water. Add salt and a handful of flour. Stir well. Sprinkle meal over top of mixture (use about ½ cup meal); let stand overnight in a warm place and

IN THE MORNING ADD:

1 cup buttermilk	1 teaspoon soda
1 cup sugar	1 teaspoon salt
	1 egg

Add meal to make a thick batter. Place in greased pan in a warm place. Let batter rise to top of pan. Bake slowly in a 350° oven for 1 hour. Use large pyrex pan for baking.

1 egg
1 cup milk
1 teaspoon baking powder

1 cup corn meal
1 teaspoon salt
Shortening, lump size of egg

Corn Meal Pancakes
Southern

Melt the shortening. Mix all the ingredients together. The batter should be very thin. Sometimes it is necessary to add a little more milk. Drop a generous tablespoon of batter on hot griddle. Serve with orange sauce.

---

1 cup corn meal
1½ cups boiling water

½ cup cold water
Pinch of salt

Fried Hasty Pudding
Southern

Add salt to boiling water. Mix corn meal with cold water. Add to the boiling water and stir constantly, cooking it until a very thick mush. Pour it out in a small loaf pan. Let cool overnight in refrigerator. Slice in ½ inch pieces and fry on a generously buttered grill until a golden brown. Serve with corned beef.

2½ cups flour
½ cup canned pumpkin
½ teaspoon salt
1 tablespoon sugar

1 teaspoon baking powder
2½ tablespoons shortening
½ cup milk

Pumpkin Biscuits
Southern

Sift flour with salt, sugar and baking powder. Cut in shortening. Add milk and mix just until all dry ingredients are moist and dough clings together. Turn out on floured board and knead slightly. Roll out to about ½ inch thickness and cut. Bake in a 450° oven for 15 minutes. Before baking, if you will brush the tops of the biscuits with water they will brown nicely.

Into 1 pint waterground corn meal, mix 1 teaspoon salt and piece of lard the size of an egg. When lard is rubbed in thoroughly, scald mixture, using only enough boiling water to moisten sufficiently to mould. Pick up by handfuls, press, leaving imprints of fingers on top, and bake in moderate oven for about ½ hour. These should be crusty with soft insides.

Corn Pone
Southern

---

4 cups mixed wild tender greens
  Dandelion
  Lamb's quarters
  Sorrel
  Chickweed
  Purslane
3 spring onions, chopped or ramps

8 nasturtium flowers
6 tablespoons oil
2 tablespoons vinegar
Salt and black pepper to taste
3 tablespoons hot bacon drippings
Juice of 1 lemon

Wild Greens and Nasturtium Salad
Southern

Mix all together, adding hot bacon drippings and lemon juice last. Serve immediately.

Jelly Pie
Southern

1 unbaked pie shell
4 egg whites, beaten
4 egg yolks, beaten
½ cup strawberry jelly or currant

½ cup butter
1½ cups sugar
1 teaspoon lemon juice

Cream butter. Add sugar gradually and beat well. Add yolks and jelly and fold in the whites of the eggs which have been stiffly beaten. Mix in lemon juice and pour in pie shell. Bake in a 350° oven for 30 minutes or until done. Serve with whipped cream.

Soup Bean Pie
Appalachian

2 cups cooked navy beans
1 cup sugar
½ cup milk

2 eggs
¼ teaspoon nutmeg
Unbaked pie crust

Run beans through a colander to remove husks. Add other ingredients, blending well. Pour into unbaked pie shell. Bake in a 375° oven for 10 minutes. Reduce heat to 325° and bake until pie is set.

Irish Potato Pie
Appalachian

1 pound potatoes peeled and cut up
1 stick butter, melted
½ teaspoon cinnamon
¼ pound sugar
½ teaspoon lemon extract

3 eggs
Juice of 1 lemon
1 cup sweet milk
1 teaspoon baking powder
Unbaked pie shell

Boil potatoes and mash fine. Mix well with butter and milk. Beat eggs and sugar together and add them to potatoes. Then add the cinnamon, extract and lemon juice. Add last the baking powder. Pour into large unbaked pie shell and bake in a 350° oven until set.

Sweet Potato Pudding
Southern

2½ cups grated raw sweet potatoes
1 cup molasses
2 eggs
2 cups rich milk
1 tablespoon butter, melted

1 teaspoon ground ginger or orange rind
1 tablespoon brown sugar
½ teaspoon powdered cinnamon

Blend all ingredients well. Bake in a 350° oven for 45 minutes or until firm. Serve with whipped cream.

Boiled Cider Pie
Southern

1 cup sugar
2 tablespoons flour
1 cup water
1 cup boiled cider

2 tablespoons melted butter
2 well-beaten eggs
1 unbaked pie shell

Blend sugar and flour. Stir in water and cider and beaten eggs and butter. Pour into unbaked pie shell. Bake in a 350° oven for 1 hour.

cup sugar	1 egg
cup milk	2 Tbs. melted butter
tsp vanilla	2 scant cup flour
dash of salt	

Poor Man's Pudding
Southern

Whip the egg. Add sugar and beat fluffy. Fold in flour and milk alternately. Pour in greased pan and bake. Bake in 350⁰ oven 45 minutes. Serve hot Lemon or Vanilla sauce.

---

lb dried apples	4 cups water
3/4 cup sugar	cinnamon and nutmeg to taste
Plain biscuit dough	

Fried Apple Pie
Southern

Cook apples and water over low heat overnight or until done and thick. Add sugar and spices.

Roll biscuit dough thin. Cut into 5 inch rounds. Place a dab of dried fruit filling on each round and fold over and crimp to seal. Fry in hot oil until crisp and brown. Drain on paper towels.

1/4 cup melted shortening	1/2 cup sugar
3 eggs	1 cup molasses
1/8 teaspoon lemon juice	1 cup broken pecans

Molasses Stick-Tight Pie
Southern

Beat all ingredients together. Pour into unbaked pie shell. Bake 45 minutes at 350 degrees.

---

eggs	1 cup brown sugar
stick butter or margarine (1/2 cup)	1/2 cup karo or molasses
cup oats	1/2 cup coconut
1/2 cup nuts	1 unbaked pie shell

Oatmeal Pie
Southern

Pour in unbaked pie shell. Bake 35 minutes at 350⁰.

---

quarts persimmons	1 teaspoon allspice
cups sour milk	½ teaspoon nutmeg
eggs, beaten	2 cups flour
cup sweet milk	1 teaspoon soda
cups brown sugar	½ pound butter, melted
teaspoon cinnamon	

Persimmon Pudding
Southern

Mash persimmons through a colander. Add sour milk. Add other ingredients in order, blending well. Bake in a well buttered baking pan in a 350° oven for 45 minutes or until firm. Serve with whipped cream.

---

cup brown sugar	1 cup nuts
1/4 cup milk	1 teaspoon vanilla
cup flour	1 teaspoon butter (melted)
teaspoon baking powder	

Brown Sugar Pudding
Southern

Mix all ingredients. Pour in pyrex baking dish. Then pour a mixture of 1 cup brown sugar and 1½ cups hot water over the pudding. Bake at 375° for 30 minutes or until brown. Serve with whipped cream.

1 cup flour	2 t baking powder
1/4 t soda	2 T shortening
1/2 t salt	1/2 cup buttermilk

Black Berry Dutch Babies
Appalachian

Sift together dry ingredients. Mix in shortening. Add milk to make dough. Divide dough into two parts and roll out each to the size of a plate. Drain juice from 1 qt. of black berries. Put 1/3 of black berries on each piece of dough. Add 2 T sugar to each. Roll up Dutch Babies and place in oblong baking pan. Pour juice from berries over Dutch Babies. Sprinkle with 1/2 cup brown sugar. Bake at 425⁰ for about 40 minutes.

Sauce

2 c brown sugar	1/2 t salt
2 rounded T flour	1 cup boiling water
4 T butter	

Combine ingredients and cook stirring constantly until thickened. Add 1/2 of sauce to Dutch Babies when baked and remaining sauce when served.

It was called "Come Back Cake" because the children always came back for more.

1 lb dried tart apples	2 t cinnamon
1 cup brown sugar	1/2 t cloves
1/2 cup white sugar	1/2 t allspice

Mash and cook apples until tender - mash thoroughly. Add sugar and spices and cool.

Stack Cake
or
"Come Back Cake"
Appalachian

Cake

4 cups flour, unsifted	1 t salt
1 cup sugar	2 eggs
4 t B. P.	1/2 cup soft butter
1/2 t soda	1 cup buttermilk
2 t vanilla	

Sift 3 3/4 cups flour into bowl. Add remaining ingredients in order given - Mix quickly and thoroughly into soft dough. Divide into parts. Use remaining 1/4 cup flour to roll out dough. Bake in 9 inch cake pans at 450⁰ until slightly brown. As you take the cake from the oven spread each layer with the apple mixture. Do not put apples on the top layer. Place in a covered container for at least 12 hours before cutting.

Cornmeal Pudding
Appalachian

1 quart milk	½ cup molasses
½ cup cornmeal	½ teaspoon cinnamon
1 tablespoon butter	½ teaspoon ginger
1 egg, well beaten	1 cup milk
¼ cup sugar	

Add cornmeal to scalding hot milk, stirring constantly. Heat to boiling and boil until thickened, about 10 minutes. Mix in butter, egg, sugar, light molasses, cinnamon and ginger. Pour into well buttered 1½ quart casserole and bake for ½ hour in a slow oven, 300°. Next add the 1 cup cold milk, stir and continue baking for 1½ hours longer.

Chess Cake
Appalachian

1 box brown sugar	**2 cups flour, sifted**
1/2 cup sugar	**1 teaspoon baking powder**
1/2 lb. butter	**1/4 teaspoon salt**
1 cup pecans, chopped	**1 teaspoon vanilla**
4 eggs	

Cream brown sugar, sugar, butter. Mix in the rest of the ingredients. Bake in 300 degree oven for 30 to 40 minutes.

1 cup sugar
¼ cup butter
1 egg
½ cup milk

1½ cups flour
2 teaspoons baking powder
½ cup cocoa
1 cup nuts

Chocolate Nut Drop Cookies
Southern

Cream sugar and butter and add egg and milk. Then add dry ingredients. Fold in nuts and drop on greased cookie sheet with teaspoon, leaving 1 inch between cookies. Bake in 375° oven for 15 minutes. P.S. Black walnuts are out of this world.

---

1 unbaked pie shell
1 cup sugar
2 heaping tablespoons flour

Milk
½ stick butter
Nutmeg

Sugar Pie
Appalachian

Put sugar in pie shell. Add flour. Blend sugar and flour with fingers. Add milk, blending with fingers so as not to puncture pie crust, until the pie shell is about ¾ full. Cut butter in tiny pieces over milk. Sprinkle generously with nutmeg. Bake at 400° until pie is set. Approximately 35 minutes.

---

1 egg
¾ cup sugar
2 tablespoons flour
1¼ teaspoons baking powder

⅛ teaspoon salt
½ cup chopped nuts
½ cup chopped apples
1 teaspoon vanilla

Mountain Pudding
Appalachian

Beat egg and sugar until thick and lemon colored. Add other ingredients. Bake in buttered pyrex dish at 350° for 35 minutes. Top with whipped cream.

---

3 cups flour
1 cup brown sugar
¾ cup butter
1 cup molasses

1 cup hot water
1 teaspoon baking soda
Few drops vinegar

Shoo-Fly Pie
Southern

Blend flour, sugar and butter until lumpy and save for topping. Blend molasses, hot water, soda and vinegar. Pour mixture into pie crusts, not baked. Top with crumb mixture and bake in a 350° oven for 35 minutes. This makes 2 pies.

SYRUP:
½ cup vinegar
1 cup sugar

1 stick margarine
½ teaspoon nutmeg
1 cup water

Vinegar Dumplings
Appalachian

Bring to a boil. Drop dumplings into mixture and boil about 15 minutes or until syrup is thick.

DUMPLINGS:
1 cup flour
2 teaspoons baking powder

½ teaspoon salt
2 tablespoons butter
6 tablespoons milk

Mix all together well like biscuit dough. Roll out into small rounds ½-inch thick and drop in vinegar syrup.

⅓ cup shortening (at room temperature)
¾ cup sweet milk
1 teaspoon salt
4 teaspoons baking powder

1 egg
1 tablespoon sugar
Flour enough to make soft dough

Apple Dumplings
Southern

Cream shortening. Add milk, salt, baking powder, egg and sugar and enough flour to make a dough. Roll dough ¼ inch thick. Cover with slices of apples and bits of butter. Roll like jelly roll and cut in pieces about 1½ inches thick. Drop into hot sauce and bake 30 to 40 minutes.

SAUCE:
1 cup sugar
3 cups boiling water

4 tablespoons flour
4 tablespoons butter
2 teaspoons nutmeg

Mix sugar, flour and nutmeg. Add water and bring to a boil. Add butter. Pour over dumplings and bake in a 350° oven until done.

1 cup sugar
2 tablespoons butter

⅛ teaspoon salt
2 cups hot water

Caramelize ½ cup of sugar until melted in a heavy sauce pan over low heat. Add rest of ingredients and let come to a boil. Drop dumplings into hot syrup. Cover and cook for 18 minutes slowly.

Caramel Dumplings
Southern

BATTER FOR DUMPLINGS:
2 tablespoons butter
1½ cups flour
½ cup sugar

2 teaspoons baking powder
½ cup milk
½ teaspoon vanilla

Cream butter and sugar. Sift dry ingredients and add alternately to butter and sugar mixture with milk. Add vanilla and stir only until blended. Drop by spoonfuls into syrup. Be sure to cover pan as they cook and only have syrup simmering. Serve with a dash of whipped cream.

6 cups thin sliced tomatoes
1 cup sugar
3 tablespoons flour
1/4 teaspoon salt
1/4 teaspoon ground cinnamon

1/4 teaspoon nutmeg
1/8 teaspoon ground cloves
1 tablespoon grated lemon peel
1/4 cup fresh lemon juice
2 tablespoons butter

Green Tomato Pie
Appalachian

Cover tomatoes with boiling water and let stand for 3 minu and drain. Mix all ingredients and put in an unbaked pie sh Bake in 350 degree oven for 35 to 40 minutes.

6 apples
1 cup light brown sugar
½ teaspoon nutmeg
1 cup warm water

Butter
Biscuit dough
1 teaspoon cinnamon

Apple Pan Dowdy
Southern

Peel and quarter apples. Put into baking dish. Sprinkl with sugar, nutmeg and cinnamon. Add water and dot wit butter. Cover apples with biscuits. Bake at 300° for 2 hours

Take a cup er brown sugar, dark brown, an'stir in six tablespoons er melted butter, a good pinch er salt, two tablespoons er peanut butter, two beat up aigs an' three cups er bran. Mix all the 'grediums thorough an'then drap on buttered pans with a teaspoon. Don't put yo macarooms too clost together kase they have a way er spreadin' like bad news. Sprinkle on top er each little cookey some grated peanuts an' then bake 'em in a hottish oven. Be keerful when you lift'em out er the pans kase they air ticklish things ter handle. The chilluns won't have no trouble gittin' away with 'em, howsomever.

These here bran macarooms kinder jazzed up with peanut butter an' grated peanuts air moughty good an' the chilluns sho' do crave 'em since they don't know how good the bran air fer they innards. I done foun' out it air a fatal thing ter let chilluns or men folks know that their victuals air wholesome. It looks like it takes away all their enj'yment er the same.

Bran and Peanut Macaroons
Southern

Combine dry ingredients:

2 3/4 cup flour	1 tsp soda
1 tsp salt	2 tsp baking powder
1 tsp ginger	1 tsp cinnamon

Combine and blend:

1 egg	1 cup oil
3/4 cup honey	3/4 cup molasses

Add flour and egg mix alternately with 1 cup buttermilk.
Bake in a 300° oven 40 minutes. Sprinkle with powdered sugar

Gingerbread
Southern

---

12 large red dry corn cobs from yellow field variety*	3 pints water
	1 package powdered pectin
3 cups sugar	1 tablespoon lemon juice

*Tennessee Red Cob or Hickory Cane are the best and make the prettiest jelly.

Shell dried corn from cob. (Feed to chickens). Save cobs only for jelly. Rinse cobs and get rid of chafe. Cut in small lengths. Boil gently for 30 minutes in 3 pints of water. Remove and strain through wet jelly bag. Measure 3 cups juice. (Add water if necessary to make 3 cups.) Add pectin to juice and bring to a boil. Add lemon juice and sugar. After it comes to a boil, boil 1 to 2 full minutes until it comes to a rolling boil. Pour while hot into sterilized jelly jars.

Corn Cob Jelly
Southern

---

2 quarts quartered apples	½ teaspoon allspice
1½ cups water	½ teaspoon cinnamon
½ cup cider	¼ teaspoon cloves
2½ cups sugar	

Cook apples in water until soft. Force through a colander. Add remaining ingredients. Cook down simmering gently until thick. About 2 or 3 hours. Makes 6 six ounce glasses.

Apple Butter
Southern

Vinegar Pie
Southern

1 egg	1 tablespoon vinegar
1 tablespoon flour (heaping)	1 cup cold water
1 cup sugar	½ teaspoon nutmeg

Beat egg, flour and sugar until creamy. Add other ingredients blending well. Bake in unbaked pie crust at 400° for 10 minutes. Reduce heat and bake until custard is set, and crust is golden brown. Serve pie topped with whipped cream.

Blackberry Jam Cake
Southern

1 cup butter	3½ cups flour
2 cups sugar	1 teaspoon cloves
3 eggs	1 teaspoon allspice
1 cup sour milk with	1 teaspoon cinnamon
1 teaspoon soda added	1 tablespoon cocoa
1 cup jam, blackberry	

Cream butter and sugar. Add eggs, beating thoroughly. Then add sour milk, soda and jam. Sift spices in flour and add to mixture. Bake in a moderate oven 375°. Bake in layers or individual cakes. Ice with marshmallow icing.

Buttermilk Icing
Southern

1 cup sugar	1 tablespoon white karo
½ cup buttermilk	¼ to ½ cup margarine
½ teaspoon soda	½ teaspoon vanilla

Combine all ingredients and cook until mixture forms a soft ball in cold water. Pour over cake without beating. Leave cake in pan until ready to serve. Cut in squares.

Cantaloupe Pie
Southern

1 medium-sized cantaloupe	½ cup sugar
(perfectly ripe)	½ stick margarine
1 rounded teaspoon flour	¼ teaspoon nutmeg

Peel cantaloupe, remove seeds and cut up in small pieces. Place in unbaked pie shell. Sprinkle flour, sugar, nutmeg and chunks of margarine over cantaloupe. Top with crust and bake at 350 for 15 minutes. Reduce heat to 300° and bake 30 minutes longer or until brown.

Cracker Pudding
Southern

1 cup crackers (crushed)	1 cup milk
1 cup water	1 egg
1 cup syrup	½ teaspoon nutmeg
4 tablespoons shortening	½ cup dry coconut

Bring water, syrup and shortening to a boil. Stir in cracker crumbs. Stir until thick. Remove from fire. Mix in remaining ingredients, beating until well blended. Bake in pyrex dish for 30 minutes in a 350° oven. Serve with vanilla sauce.

If Power Fails

A good way to cook if you do not have a fireplace is to take a roll of toilet tissue and soak it with rubbing or denatured alcohol. Place in an empty Crisco tin that has a lid. Set can on bricks and build up sides around can with bricks to hold skillet. Remove lid from can and light. Smother fire with lid each time you have finished cooking. This makes a great cooking fire for hunters, too.

1 gallon rain water
1 pint shelled Indian corn

Boil water and corn together until kernels burst.

Pour into a 2 gallon stone jug and add enough filtered rain water to make jug half full (replace that which evaporated from boiling).

Dissolve
½ pound of sugar in 1 cup clear rain water by bringing to a boil. Pour into jug and stir or shake well.

Cover the mouth of jug with 2 or 3 thicknesses of cheese cloth. Let stand in warm place, 75 to 80 degrees, for 1 month.

Pour off this vinegar into another jug, leaving half the mother and repeat process.

To preserve this vinegar, cover the mouth of the jug with a piece of cloth and store in a dry warm place.

This is excellent vinegar.

Corn Vinegar
Southern

---

24 small fresh pods of okra or or 2 packages whole frozen okra	½ cup vinegar
Juice of 2 lemons	3 tablespoons finely minced onions
2 cloves chopped garlic	3 tablespoons chopped red and
1 cup oil	green bell pepper
	1 tablespoon fresh chopped parsley

Boil okra until tender. Drain and squeeze fresh lemon juice over okra. Chill in refrigerator.
To serve place 4 okra pods on leaf lettuce. Combine the remaining ingredients and shake well. Serve with the oil and vinegar dressing.

Okra Salad
Southern

---

1 gallon vinegar	1 pound brown sugar
1 cup salt	2 ounces black pepper
2 ounces ginger	2 ounces white mustard seed
2 ounces ground mustard	2 ounces celery seed
1 ounce tumeric	2 ounces whole cloves
1 cup grated horseradish	

Fresh chopped onions, cucumber, celery, cabbage, greentomatoes, red and green pepers, beans, carrots, etc.

Put vinegar in 2 gallon crock jar. Add sugar and spices. Add vegetables until crock is almost full. Be sure vinegar covers the vegetables well. Weight down with plate and let stand for 2 weeks before using.

Crock Jug Pickle Relish
(No Cooking)
Southern

---

12 ears corn	1 pint mustard
1 medium head cabbage, ground	2 pints vinegar
12 medium-sized onions, ground	½ cup salt
6 bell peppers, ground	2½ cups sugar
2 or 3 red peppers	

Cut corn off cob, but do not scrape. Boil corn in vinegar for 20 minutes. Add rest of ingredients and boil 10 minutes longer. Seal while hot in jars. Makes 6 pints.

Corn Relish
Southern

Ripe Tomato Relish
Southern

1 peck ripe tomatoes, cubed
2 hot red peppers, broken
6 bell peppers, chopped
1 cup celery, chopped
3 large onions, chopped

1 cup salt
2 pounds brown sugar
1 quart vinegar
3 teaspoons cinnamon
2 teaspoons dry mustard

Mix all ingredients together with salt. Tie up in a muslin sack and let drain for 3 hours. Do not use liquid that drains off. Be careful not to mash tomatoes when mixing. Heat sugar, vinegar, cinnamon and dry mustard only until sugar is dissolved. Pour over tomato-vegetable mixture, mixing well. Seal up in jars.

Old Fashioned Mincemeat
Southern

Take 2 pounds of tender beef, 1½ pounds of suet, 4 pounds chopped green apples, 1½ pound currants, washed dried and picked, 1½ pounds seeded raisins, 3 pounds of white sugar, 1 pound citron cut thin, the grating, juice and pulp of 1 orange, the juice and grated rinds of 2 lemons, ½ ounce of cinnamon, ⅛ ounce each of cloves, mace and allspice, 2 nutmegs grated, 1 pint of madiera wine, ½ pint brandy, ½ cup strawberry preserves. Boil the meat in the smallest amount of water possible. Chop fine. After removing the membrane from suet, dredge with flour and chop very fine. Mix it through the meat with salt to remove fresh taste. To this add the apples, sugar, fruit, spice and other ingredients. Add a little sweet cider or molasses and salt to taste. This mincemeat is not to be cooked. Store in cool place until ready to use.

Mincemeat Turnovers
Southern

Flaky pastry
⅔ cup mincemeat
⅔ cup chopped apples

⅓ cup walnuts
3 tablespoons lemon juice

Roll pastry in 5 inch rounds. Combine rest of ingredients and spoon on rounds. Seal edges together with a little water. Make a slit in top of each turnover. Bake in a 350° oven until done.

Chow Chow
Southern

1 gallon chopped cabbage
12 onions
12 green peppers (sweet)
12 red peppers (sweet)
2 quarts chopped green tomatoes
5 cups sugar
4 tablespoons ground mustard

1 tablespoon tumeric
1 tablespoon ground ginger
4 tablespoons mustard seed
3 tablespoons celery seed
2 tablespoons mixed whole spices
2 to 3 quarts vinegar

Chop onion and peppers. Mix all vegetables with ½ cup salt. Let stand overnight. Drain. Tie the mixed spices in a bag. Add sugar and spices to the vinegar. Simmer for 20 minutes. Add all of the other ingredients and simmer until hot and well seasoned. (10 minutes). Remove the spice bag. Pack chow chow into hot sterilized jars and seal at once. Make 14 pints.

2 pounds tiny premature corncobs
1 1/2 to 2 inches long
1 pound granulated sugar
2 sticks whole cinnamon
1/2 ounce alum
1 cup white wine vinegar
1 bay leaf

Trim cobs of all silks and husks. Boil alum in 12 gallon water. Pour over cobs and let stand in a warm place for 1 hour. Drain. Chill in cold water.

Make syrup of vinegar, sugar and the spices tied in a cheese cloth bag. Bring to the boiling point and add corncobs. Cook 5 minutes. Remove spice bag. Fill sterilized jars with cobs and liquid. Seal and store in a cool dark place.

Pickled Corncobs
Southern

---

1 gallon sliced cucumbers
12 small onions, sliced
½ cup salt
Cracked ice
4 cups vinegar
4 cups sugar
1½ teaspoons tumeric
½ teaspoon cloves
1 teaspoon celery seed
2 teaspoons mustard seed

Let cucumbers and onions stand for 3 hours in salted ice water. Bring to a boil vinegar, sugar, tumeric, cloves, celery seed and mustard seed. Add cucumbers and onions. Simmer until they lose their bright color. Seal in jars.

Bread and Butter Pickles
Southern

---

5 lbs. tomatoes, red or yellow
2 lbs. sugar
1/2 teaspoon salt
1 orange, thinly sliced
1 lemon, thinly sliced
1 stick (3 inch) cinnamon
1 piece whole ginger
2 cups seedless raisins
1/2 cup lemon juice
1/4 teaspoon tabasco

Peel tomatoes and chop. Combine with sugar, salt, sliced orange and sliced lemon. Stir over heat until sugar dissolves. Add cinnamon and ginger, bring to a boil; cook over low heat until thick, about 1 hour, stirring occasionally. Remove cinnamon and ginger. Add raisins and lemon juice and bring again to a boil. Stir in tabasco, pour into hot pint or half-pint jars, and seal at once. Makes 3 1/2 pints.

Tomato Chutney
Southern

To make five gallons of brilliant stucco whitewash for buildings, inside or out, take six quarts of clean lumps of well-burnt lime; slack with hot water in a covered tub to keep in the steam. It should then be passed through a fine sieve to obtain the flower of lime; add one-fourth of a pound of burnt alum pulverized. 1 pound of sugar, 3 pints of rice flour, made into a thin well-boiled starch or jelly, add 1 pound of glue, dissolved in hot water. This may be applied warm. A whitewash thus made is said to be more brilliant than plaster of paris, and to retain its brilliancy many years. It should be put on with a common painter's brush, a second coat being applied after the first is well dried. The east end of the White House at Washington was formerly painted with this composition.

Whitewash

Potpourri Jar

Gather the blossoms early in the morning. Roses, Pinks, Lemon Verbena, Tuberoses and Violets. Strip off the leaves and petals and spread on paper to dry in the attic or in an airy unused room. When dry take a large glass bowl and for every 4 quarts of petals and leaves, use 1 cup of salt. Sprinkle ¼ cup on the bottom then 2 cups of petals, then more salt and more petals until all are used having salt for the top layer. Cover for 5 days stirring twice daily. When moist add 2 ounces of crushed allspice berries and 2 ounces of crushed stick cinnamon. Let this stand covered one week, turning daily. Now mix together:

1 ounce crushed cloves	2 ounces dried orange peel grated
2 nutmegs coarsely grated	
2 ounces ginger root sliced thin	2 ounces dried lemon peel grated
2 ounces orris root sliced thin	
½ pound dried lavender flowers	½ ounce dried rosemary

MIX WELL—Pack the petal mixture alternately with spice mixture into a little jar—when filled pour over it 1 pint of cologne. Cover closely. Shake and stir ever few days. Place potpourri jars in rooms. Lift off the top for a few minutes each day to keep your house smelling sweet.

No-Rinse Cleaning Solution for Walls

Put 1 gallon of hot water into a galvanized steel pail, add 1 cup of household ammonia, ½ cup of vinegar and ¼ cup of baking soda to the water. Mix thoroughly and you have a solution that cleans walls quickly without any need of rinsing. You can use a sponge or soft cloth for the washing. Wash a small area at a time. That's all there is to it. No rinsing needed. Be sure and work from the bottom of the wall up then you will have no streaks from the water dripping over a dirty space. Water will streak a dirty wall but does not streak a clean wall.

Life is so sweet, because of the friends we have made,
    And the things that in common we share;
We want to live on, not because of ourselves,
    But because of the people who care.
It is giving and doing for somebody else —
    Upon that life's splendor depends;
And the joy of the world, when we sum it all up,
    I find, is the making of friends.

Down on the Farm Remedies

To cleanse the body and stimulate the liver, drink a cup of beet, celery, lettuce, carrot or apple juice.

Sleep Inducer - 1 glass buttermilk with 2 tablespoons honey and juice of 1 lemon.

Water is the world's best medicine. A cold bath is a great tonic. While in the country, bathe in a cold creek.

Chew honeysuckle blossoms to chase the blues away.

To keep flies away, sprinkle oil of sassafras or oil of lavender around room.

Flies don't like onions or kerosene either. Try wiping your screens with kerosene rags and notice how this clears the flies away.

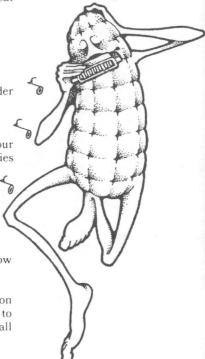

Charcoal removes musty odors.

Stings - Mix honey and soda to a salve. Cover sting and allow to dry.

Cure for warts and corns - Lemon juice or pick a dandelion flower or leaf. Squeeze the juice out on wart or corn. Allow to dry. Repeat 3 days. The wart or corn will turn dark and fall off.

Hot or Cold - 1 tablespoon honey and 3/4 cup boiling water makes a soothing eye wash, or try closing the eyes and using a compress of cold honey-water pads for swollen eyes.

Cooked oatmeal and okra are soothing foods for any stomach ailment.

Home made cough syrup:
Mix 1/2 cup honey, 3 Tbs. apple cider vinegar, 1 Tbs. butter, dash of red hot pepper. Heat and take 1 tsp as needed for cough or hoarsness.

Cough Syrup

Dandelion Wine (Bottled Sunshine)
or
Clover Blossom Wine

Pick
  1 gallon dandelion or clover blossoms in the morning when the dew is still on them.

Put into a 2 gallon crock and cover with boiling water. Spread cheesecloth over container and let set at room temperature for 3 days. Squeeze juice out. Put this into an enamel pot and add 3 pounds of light brown sugar, 4 lemons sliced and 2 oranges sliced. Put a lid on the pot and boil for 30 minutes. Let cool to lukewarm. Pour solution back into the crock. Add 2 packages of yeast. Cover the container and let ferment 2 or 3 weeks or until it stops bubbling. Filter through cheesecloth.

I have been told you can tie a big balloon on a small mouth jar and watch balloon expand. When it deflates after several weeks, the wine is ready.

Concord Grape Wine
Southern

Wash and mash fully ripened grapes. Put into earthen crock, keg or barrel according to amount of grapes used. Add a small amount of sugar to start fermentation (1 1/2 lbs. per barrel would be sufficient). Let stand from 5 to 7 days depending on the temperature. If the mixture is kept in a cool place, it would possibly take 7 days, in moderate temperature, six days and if the weather is extremely warm, 5 days would be sufficient. Draw the juice off from the bottom of the container, press the pulp to extract the remaining juice, strain and measure. Add 2 lbs. sugar per gallon. If a keg or barrel is used, place a tube in the "bung" at the top of keg, seal around the tube to close out any air, place the end of the tube into a container of water. This allows the gas to escape without air getting to the wine. It will take approximately 90 days for fermentation to cease. When it stops bubbling, remove the tube and seal the container with a stopper. With smaller amounts made in a crock, the juice can be put into jugs or bottles after the sugar is added. Put the caps on the bottles and loosen one turn to let the gas escape. When it quits working, seal the container.

Elder Blossom Wine
Southern

1 quart elder blossoms, washed and
  picked from stems
3 pounds raisins
9 pounds sugar
3 lemons (sliced)
1 cake yeast
3 gallons boiling water

Use a crock or similar container (no metal). Pour boiling water over the elder blossoms, raisins, sugar and lemons. Stir to dissolve sugar. When luke warm, put in 1 cake yeast and stir up the sugar again. Let stand for 24 hours. Strain and pour into bottles. Seal with caps and loosen 1 turn to let gas escape. When fermentation has ceased, tighten caps completely. This will make approximately 3 1/2 gallons.

7 Day Diet

Day 1 -   Eat all the fresh fruit you want
Day 2 -   Eat all the fresh vegetables you want, even 1 small baked
           potato, no butter.
Day 3 -   Eat fruits and vegetables (no potato).
Day 4 -   Eat 8 bananas, 8 glasses of skim milk.
Day 5 -   10 ounces beef, 6 whole tomatoes.
Day 6 -   10 ounces beef and fresh vegetables (no potato).
Day 7 -   Brown rice and vegetables, eat all you want.

Between meals or anytime you are hungry eat the following soup.

Diet Soup

6 large onions	1 bunch celery
3 bell peppers	1 package dry onion soup mix
1 head cabbage	2 large cans tomato juice

Chop vegetables and add tomato juice and soup mix. Simmer until vegetables are done. Store in refrigerator and use when needed.

Beauty Treatments and Hints

1.   Add 1 cup powdered milk to bath water for smooth skin.

2.   If skin is oily rinse skin in milk solution of soda water. 1/4
      tsp to 1 cup warm water.

3.   To remove wrinkles:
      Mix 1/2 tsp honey, 1/2 tsp rose water, 1 egg white, 1 tsp
      milk and 2 tsp cucumber juice. Keep mixture in jar in
      refrigerator. Apply to face with cotton pads. Let dry 20
      minutes and then rinse. You will feel 20 years younger.

4.   Tomato juice will remove skunk scent from your pets
      and from your cloths.

5.   If your hair is getting thin, take equal parts of green tea
      and garden sage and three parts of boiling water. Boil
      down and strain and apply to scalp night and morning.
      This will stimulate growth.

6.   For pretty glossy hair, rinse in tea or 1 egg mixed with 1
      oz of water.

7.   To make your own apple cider vinegar:
      Put 1 gallon of warm water in big earthern jar. Add 2
      cups sugar and 1 package of yeast. Add peelings from red
      apples. Stir and let stand for about 1 month. Vinegar will
      be ready a little sooner if the weather is warm.

I wish you health, money and love and the time to
enjoy them.
      Proverb

Energy Saving Tips

Use pans with tight-fitting lids and with flat bottoms that fit the surface unit.

Cook foods at the lowest possible heat and with the least amount of water.

Don't peek! Time food when cooking so heat is not lost by opening the oven door or lifting a lid.

Thaw foods completely before cooking.

Use the oven for cooking food, not for heating the kitchen.

Preheat the oven for baked goods only. It does not have to be preheated for casseroles, roasting meat or for broiling.

Cook entire meals in the oven. Make a double quantity and freeze the extra portion.

Bake in glass or ceramic dishes and reduce oven temperature by 25 degrees F.

Keep surface unit reflector pans and oven clean for more efficient operation.

Turn off the oven or surface units 3-5 minutes before food is done. Food will continue to cook.

During warm weather try to cook in the coolest part of the day and prepare foods that need no cooking, when possible.

Do not overcook foods. This wastes energy and food value.

When baking in aluminum foil, turn the dull side to the outside.

When possible, use small appliances or the microwave oven for more energy efficient cooking.

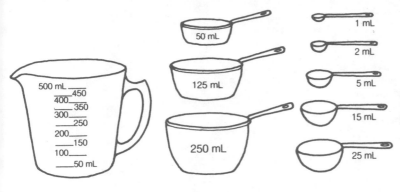

Metric measures are much like
customary types, even quantities.
Smallest (1 mL) spoon holds about
¼ teaspoon; top line on big cup
marks 500 mL, or about 2 cups.

Sweetpeas Tulips	Plunge stems into boiling water then into cold water.
Violets	Tie in bunches and submerge in water; then shake off all water.
Zinnia	Stripped of lower leaves, place in 2 quarts of water containing 2 tablespoons of rock salt.
Snapdragons	Place stems, stripped of lower leaves in two quarts water containing 3 tablespoons of baking soda.
Cat Tails	Cut with few leaves about August 25th. Place in vase upright, no water.
Pansies	Place stems in 1 pint of water containing 5 drops of wood alcohol.
Peonies	Crush stem ends up 3 to 4 inches and place in two quarts of water containing 2 teaspoonsful of sugar.
Poppies	Char stem tips two to three inches over a hot flame and plunge into cold water.
Ranunculas	Add vinegar to the water, at the rate of 1/2 cup vinegar to 2 cups water.
Roses	Slit the stem up 2 inches and place in two quarts of water containing 5 drops of wood alcohol.

Pumpkin Pie Cake

1 can (1 lb. 13 oz.) pumpkin
1 can (13 oz.) evaporated milk
3 eggs, slightly beaten
1½ teaspoons cinnamon
¼ teaspoon cloves
½ teaspoon nutmeg

¼ teaspoon ginger
½ teaspoon salt
1 cup sugar
1 box yellow cake mix
1 cup chopped nuts
1 stick butter melted

Blend together all ingredients EXCEPT last three. Pour this mixture into 13x9x2-inch pan. Sprinkle evenly with yellow cake mix and chopped nuts. Drizzle melted butter over all. Bake at 350 degrees about 50 minutes. Serve with whipped cream.

Peanut Butter Cake

(With Peanut Butter Broiled Frosting)

¾ cup shortening
¾ cup peanut butter
2¼ cups brown sugar
1½ teaspoon vanilla
3 eggs

2¼ cups sifted cake flour
¾ teaspoon salt
3 teaspoons baking powder
1 cup milk

Cream shortening, peanut butter and sugar. Add eggs and vanilla. Beat well. Sift flour with salt and baking powder. Add alternately with milk, adding the dry ingredients first and last. Pour batter into greased 13x9x2-inch pan. Bake in a moderate oven of 350° F. for 50 minutes.

Peanut Butter Broiled Frosting

Cream 6 tablespoons butter or margarine, 1 cup brown sugar, and ⅔ cup peanut butter. Add ¼ cup milk and stir well. The add ⅔ cup chopped peanuts and spread over warm cake. Place under broiler and broil a few minutes until bubbly.

Crusty Water Bread

1 envelope of yeast
¼ cup warm water

Soften yeast in warm water.
In a mixing bowl combine:

> **2 egg whites**
> **1 teaspoon salt**
> **1 tablespoon sugar**
> **1 cup warm water**

> Beat until stiff.

Add 4 cups flour and 2 tablespoons oil. Continue to beat with dough hook until smooth and elastic. Brush dough with oil. Let rise 1 hour. Punch down let rise 45 minutes longer. Shape into 2 long loaves. Place on pan, brush with oil, cover and let rise until double bake in 350° oven 1 hour. For extra thick crust, place pan of warm water in oven while baking.

Seafood Gumbo

6 tablespoons flour
½ cup butter
6 cloves garlic, chopped
½ cup diced onions
¼ cup chopped green bell pepper
½ cup chopped celery
2 pounds peeled *raw* shrimp
1-8 ounce can tomato sauce
3 quarts water
1 pound crabmeat or lobster
¼ cup parsley, chopped
½ teaspoon thyme
3 bay leaves
1 package frozen sliced okra
1 pint oysters with juice
Salt and pepper to taste

Make a roux with flour and butter. Add garlic, onion, bell pepper and celery. Cook covered until transparent. Add water, tomato sauce and okra. Simmer until done. Add seasonings, lobster, shrimp and oysters. Simmer 30 minutes and serve.

Pickled Shrimp or Mushrooms

2 pounds shelled, deveined cooked shrimp
or
1 pound fresh white mushrooms

Marinade

1 cup vinegar
1 cup water
1 tablespoon sugar
1 chopped onion
1 bay leaf
½ teaspoon peppercorns
¼ cup red bell pepper, chopped
Seasoning salt

Mix all ingredients and marinate the mushrooms or shrimp for at least 4 hours in refrigerator.

Grapefruit Salad

1 package lime jello
½ cup hot water
1 No. 2 can grapefruit

1 9-oz. can crushed pineapple
1 small onion, if desired

Dissolve jello in hot water. Add grapefruit and pineapple and onion. Let stand until firm.

Artichokes

Hot: 1 firm artichoke per serving
Trim off base and tip of bud. Plunge into salted hot water and boil (simmering) for 45 minutes.

Serve with Hot Butter Sauce (enough for 6)
1 cup butter
1 teaspoon lemon juice
1 teaspoon herb salt
Dash white pepper

MY FAVORITE RECIPES FOR ENTERTAINING

Turkey In A Bag

Save your big brown grocery sacks for this!

(Do not use recycled paper)

Rub your turkey (or any fowl) with salad oil. Place him in paper bag and tie up with a string or skewer.

Place them on cooking pan and roast according to chart.

7-10 lbs. — 30 min. per pound
10-15 lbs. — 20 min. per pound
15-18 lbs. — 18 min. per pound
18-20 lbs. — 15 min. per pound
20-23 lbs. — 13 min. per pound

Roast in 300 degree oven.

For dressing stock and gravy boil the neck and giblets.

If you want, you may prepare a suckling pig the same way.

Roasting is easy and fail proof!

Cornbread Dressing

6 cups cornbread (crumbled)
⅓ cup chopped onion
1 cup chopped celery
2 tablespoons chopped parsley
1½ teaspoons salt
1 tablespoon poultry seasoning
1 teaspoon sage
½ teaspoon pepper
Turkey broth to moisten well
½ stick butter (melted)

Mix all ingredients. Pour into baking pan and bake 1 hour at 375 degrees. Serve with turkey gravy.

White Wine Freeze

1/2 cup sugar
1 cup water
Grated rind of 1/2 lemon

Juice of 1 lemon
2 cups medium dry, white wine
dash of angostura

Boil sugar and water. Let cool. Mix other ingredients. Freeze in hand freezer. Let stand at room temperature for 5 minutes and serve garnished with fresh raspberries and strawberries, pineapple and bananas.

Stuffed Mushrooms a la Phila

24 large mushroom caps (2-3 inches) with stems
½ stick butter
2 cups chopped mushroom stems
2 cups cubed soft light bread
3 strips of bacon chopped
1 large onion chopped or spring onions (¾ cup)
2 tablespoons tomato catsup
1 tablespoon Worcestershire sauce
¼ cup Chablis
Juice of 2 lemons

Saute bacon and onion until done but not brown, add butter and chopped mushroom stems. Saute 5 minutes. Stir in rest of ingredients blending until bread is thoroughly mixed with other ingredients. Set aside until cool enough to handle. Stuff mushrooms. Cover and bake in 350° oven 30 minutes. Dab a little sour cream over them if you reheat.

Carrot and Orange Salad

1 package orange jello
1¾ cup water
½ cup grated carrots

⅓ cup grated cheese
½ cup pineapple

Dissolve gelatin in 1¾ cup hot water. Add carrots, cheese and pineapple. Let stand until firm.

Cheese and Bacon Soup

6 strips of bacon
1 cup onion
2 cups chopped celery
2 cups grated carrots
½ cup chopped pimentos
1 pound creamy cheese spread
8 cups water or chicken broth
2 tablespoons chicken stock base
1 cup cream

Saute onion and celery with chopped bacon until soft. Add chicken broth and carrots. Simmer 10 minutes. Remove from heat and stir in cheese blending smooth. Stir in cream and keep warm, do not boil.

Stir Fry Vegetables For Flavor, Crunch

To stir fry vegetables, follow these steps:
• Cut vegetables in slices, shreds, slivers or on the bias.
• Heat two tablespoons of vegetable oil per four cups of vegetables. Add one-half teaspoon of salt and stir.
• Pour in vegetables and stir over high heat for a few seconds until well coated with oil.
• Add one-half cup liquid and stir a few seconds over high heat.
• Cover, lower heat, and simmer three to five minutes. Vegetables will still have a crunchy texture.

Southern Squash Supreme
(30 servings)

1 gallon shredded squash
1 cup shredded onion
2 tsp. black pepper
1 tablespoon salt
1 cup melted butter
1 cup flour
¼ cup cornstarch
2 tbs. sugar
4 cups milk
8 eggs slightly beaten

Mix all ingredients in order given.
Pour into 12 x 20 inch pan. Bake 45-50 minutes at 350°.

Papaya Seed Marinade

1 cup white wine vinegar
1/2 cup sugar
1 teaspoon dry mustard
1 teaspoon seasoning salt

2 cups peanut oil
1 teaspoon powdered onion
2 tablespoons fresh papaya seeds

Put vinegar and dry ingredients in mixer. Gradually add the oil, then the papaya seeds. Blend until the seeds break up like coarse pepper. Brush this over pork ribs while grilling, or serve over leaf lettuce as a dressing. It also makes a perfect dressing for avocados. Papaya seeds have a hot peppery taste.

MY FAVORITE RECIPES FOR ENTERTAINING

Roast Beef Yorkshire Pudding

1 top or bottom of round, 15-18 pounds
Salt and black pepper roast. Allow to stand until it reaches room temperature.

Roast in 350 degree oven until desired doneness (use meat thermometer). DO NOT cover while roasting and DO NOT add water to pan.

When done, remove roast from pan. Add 2 cups hot water to pan drippings. Thicken with cornstarch and water.

Yorkshire Pudding

1 cup sifted flour (pastry)
½ teaspoon salt
½ cup milk
2 eggs, separated
½ cup water
Beef drippings or ½ cup butter

Sift flour and salt into a bowl. Stir in milk. Beat until foamy. Beat egg yolks until thick and lemon colored. Beat whites until stiff. Fold in egg yolks. Beat eggs into the flour and milk batter. Add water and beat until large bubbles rise to the surface. Let stand 1 hour. Beat again. Pour into preheated butter greased baking pan. Bake in 450 degree oven for 45 minutes. Cut in squares and serve with roast beef and gravy.

Slaw

1 medium head cabbage, shredded	2 teaspoons sugar
1 medium onion, sliced thinly	2 teaspoons salt
7/8 cup sugar	1 teaspoon dry mustard
1 cup vinegar	1 teaspoon celery seed
3/4 cup salad oil	

Mix vinegar, salad oil, 2 teaspoons sugar, salt, mustard and celery seed and bring to a boil. Alternate layers of cabbage and onion rings in a large bowl. Top with 7/8 cup sugar. Pour hot mixture over cabbage and onion. Cover and let stand 4 to 6 hours. Mix well and serve. Will keep 2 to 3 weeks in refrigerator.

Time is so precious that there is never but one moment in the world at once, and that is always taken away before another is given . . . . .
Unknown Author

Boeuf Bourguignon
Beef Bourbon

2 pounds lean beef, cubed
2 tablespoons bacon drippings
5 medium sized onions, chopped
1½ tablespoons flour
1 cup dry red wine
½ pound fresh mushrooms
4 ounces bourbon whiskey
½ teaspoon thyme
Salt to taste
Pepper to taste
½ teaspoon marjoram
½ cup beef bouillon

Fry onions in bacon drippings. Remove to separate dish. Saute beef in bacon drippings. Sprinkle with flour, thyme, salt, pepper, and marjoram. Add ½ cup bouillon and 1 cup wine. Simmer 3½ hours very slowly. Add half bouillon and wine if more liquid is needed as it cooks. Add browned onions and mushrooms. Cook 30 minutes longer. Sauce should be thick and dark brown. Add 4 ounces bourbon and serve immediately.

1 cup sour cream may be added if you would like to change recipe to Stroganoff.

Potato Soufflé

3 tablespoons butter	1 cup mashed potatoes
3 tablespoons all-purpose flour	3 eggs, separated
1 cup light cream	salt and pepper
1 teaspoon minced onion	

Melt butter and blend in flour. Add cream and cook, stirring, until thickened. Add onion and potatoes; heat, stirring until hot. Stir in beaten egg yolks quickly. Season, and fold in stiffly beaten egg whites. Spoon into 1 1/2-quart souffle' dish, and bake in preheated moderate oven for 30 minutes, until puffed and firm. 4 to 6 servings.

'Spice' Fruit Torte

½ cup corn starch   ½ tsp nutmeg
½ tsp salt   1 tsp vanilla
1½ tsp baking powder   ½ cup shortening
¼ cup milk   1 cup white sugar
2 Eggs   1 cup whole wheat flour

Cream shortening, sugar and nutmeg until fluffy. Sift together flour, corn-starch, salt and baking powder. Blend Eggs with milk and vanilla—add dry ingredients alternately with milk mixture ending up with flour. Grease and flour a 9 inch torte pan. Add batter. Bake in 350° oven for about 25-30 min. Cool in pan for about 15 min. Turn out of pan and top with 1 cup sour cream mixed with 2 tablespoons of honey and 1 tablespoon of vanilla. Cool in refrigerator after topping with fresh sliced peaches, strawberries, kiwis and blueberries. Serve with whipping cream if desired.

Meringue Puffs
with Lemon Ice Box Glaze

¾ cup sugar
1 cup water   2 teaspoons flavoring
2 tablespoons cornstarch   6 egg whites, beaten, stiff, but not dry

Combine sugar, water and cornstarch. Cook until thick. Add flavoring. Set aside while beating egg whites. Pour hot, thick syrup into beaten egg whites and continue to beat until all syrup is added. With pastry tube pipe mounds onto refrigerator dish. Pour lemon ice box glaze quickly over meringues.

Lemon Ice Box Glaze

6 egg yolks
2 cans evaporated condensed milk
⅔ cup lemon juice

Beat egg yolks until fluffy. Add milk (at room temperature). Blend in lemon juice. Before it sets up, spoon over meringue puffs. Allow to stand in refrigerator until firm.

Strawberry Water Ice

1 cup water
1 cup sugar
2 tablespoons lemon juice
1 quart crushed strawberries (1½ cups)
2 stiffly beaten egg whites

Heat sugar and water until dissolved. Add lemon juice and cool. Fold in crushed strawberries and egg whites stiffly beaten. Freeze until firm.

Appetizers and Soups

Entrees

Sauces

Vegetables and Meat Accompaniments

Salads and Salad Dressing

Breads and Such

Desserts and Party Favorites

Appalachian, Mountain & Country Favorites

PHILA HACH
Official Worlds Fair Cookbook
1601 Madison St.
Clarksville, Tn. 37040

Please send _____ copies of Worlds Fair Cookbook at $9.00 per copy, postpaid.

Name _____

Street _____

City _____ State _____ Zip _____

Enclosed is check or money order for $ _____ .
Make checks payable to Phila R. Hach

PHILA HACH
Official Worlds Fair Cookbook
1601 Madison St.
Clarksville, Tn. 37040

Please send _____ copies of Worlds Fair Cookbook at $9.00 per copy, postpaid.

Name _____

Street _____

City _____ State _____ Zip _____

Enclosed is check or money order for $ _____ .
Make checks payable to Phila R. Hach

PHILA HACH
Official Worlds Fair Cookbook
1601 Madison St.
Clarksville, Tn. 37040

Please send _____ copies of Worlds Fair Cookbook at $9.00 per copy, postpaid.

Name _____

Street _____

City _____ State _____ Zip _____

Enclosed is check or money order for $ _____ .
Make checks payable to Phila R. Hach